PRAISE FOR *WITH ALL D*

With All Due Respect

With All Due Respect

40 DAYS TO A MORE FULFILLING RELATIONSHIP WITH YOUR TEENS AND TWEENS

NINA ROESNER AND DEBBIE HITCHCOCK

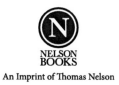

NELSON
BOOKS

An Imprint of Thomas Nelson

Published in Nashville, Tennessee, by Nelson Books, an imprint of Thomas Nelson. Nelson Books and Thomas Nelson are registered trademarks of HarperCollins Christian Publishing, Inc.

Thomas Nelson titles may be purchased in bulk for educational, business, fund-raising, or sales promotional use. For information, please e-mail SpecialMarkets@ThomasNelson.com.

Unless otherwise noted, Scripture quotations are taken from THE HOLY BIBLE, NEW INTERNATIONAL VERSION®, NIV® Copyright © 1973, 1978, 1984, 2011 by Biblica, Inc.® Used by permission. All rights reserved worldwide.

Scripture quotations marked NKJV are from THE NEW KING JAMES VERSION. Copyright © 1982 by Thomas Nelson, Inc. Used by permission. All rights reserved.

Scripture quotations marked ESV are from The Holy Bible, English Standard Version® (ESV®), copyright © 2001 by Crossway, a publishing ministry of Good News Publishers. Used by permission. All rights reserved.

Scripture quotations marked AMP are from THE AMPLIFIED BIBLE. Copyright © 2015 by The Lockman Foundation, La Habra, CA 90631. All rights reserved.

Scripture quotations marked NLT are from the Holy Bible, New Living Translation. © 1996, 2004, 2007, 2013 by Tyndale House Foundation. Used by permission of Tyndale House Publishers, Inc., Carol Stream, Illinois 60188. All rights reserved.

Scripture quotations marked NASB are from NEW AMERICAN STANDARD BIBLE®, © 1960, 1962, 1963, 1968, 1971, 1972, 1973, 1975, 1977, 1995 by The Lockman Foundation. Used by permission. (www.Lockman.org)

Scripture quotations marked KJV are from the King James Version of the Bible.

Any Internet addresses, phone numbers, or company or product information printed in this book are offered as a resource and are not intended in any way to be or to imply an endorsement by Thomas Nelson, nor does Thomas Nelson vouch for the existence, content, or services of these sites, phone numbers, companies, or products beyond the life of this book.

ISBN 978-0-718-08148-5 (e-book)

Library of Congress Cataloging-in-Publication Data

ISBN 978-0-718-08147-8

Printed in the United States of America

16 17 18 19 20   RRD   10 9 8 7 6 5 4 3 2 1

FOR OUR FAMILIES

From Nina

Special thanks to my husband, Jim Roesner, who chairs Greater Impact's board of directors and has been my life partner since 1991. I can't imagine what it is like for you to be married to me! This journey has been a surprise to us both. I'm especially thankful for the children He's blessed our marriage with—you know we wouldn't have any of them were it not for you!

Adam, Bram, and Lizzie: thank you for all your cheering, celebrating, support, and encouragement in this writing career. I love you all to pieces and am just so thankful God brought you into my life.

From Debbie

Dave, we've both grown so much as we've been on this parenting rollercoaster. What a wild ride we've encountered! I love you all the more for actively choosing to join forces to do this parenting gig together. Thank you for all you do, from reading manuscripts and adding insight to supporting me in every way. Thanks especially for helping with laundry duty and last minute meal preparation! You truly are my best friend.

Matt, Andrea, Drew, and Michael: you've challenged my thinking in ways I never dreamed possible. It is by the grace of God that I finally learned the true meaning of respect as I parented each of you. You were the ones who encouraged me to take this leap of faith in writing and training parents! Thanks for holding me accountable to completion. I'm blessed to call you my sons and daughter.

Early the next morning they arose and worshiped before the LORD and then went back to their home at Ramah. Elkanah made love to his wife Hannah, and the LORD remembered her. So in the course of time Hannah became pregnant and gave birth to a son. She named him Samuel, saying "Because I asked the LORD for him." . . .

"I prayed for this child, and the LORD has granted me what I asked of him. So now I give him to the LORD. For his whole life he will be given over to the LORD."

—1 SAMUEL 1:19–20, 27–28

CONTENTS

WHAT YOU NEED TO KNOW BEFORE YOU GET STARTED

A Note from Nina . . .

You may have stumbled upon this book after getting to know us through *The Respect Dare* or Greater Impact's Daughters of Sarah® course. Maybe you've already read some of the awesome parenting books out there, and this is just another step in your journey. Maybe you are feeling overwhelmed, scared, and insecure about what to do with your tweens and teens, and are hoping this book can give you the wisdom and tools you need to be a better mom.

However you got here, know you are not alone.

This is a book written for moms of tweens and teens. All of the stories fit in this age range. While we are aware of the very important impact a fully engaged dad can have on his family, we realize that moms, on average, spend more time with their kids than dads do. So our focus is on the mom, though we will discuss and give examples of kids' interactions with their dad and parenting within the family. However, this book is intended to speak to those of you on the front lines, to help you in your mothering as you navigate the hormone-drenched awkward waters of adolescence. We realize a number of the moms we minister to find themselves co-parenting with an ex-husband, dealing with blended family issues, or making the parenting journey without a spouse. Because the majority of the women we minister to online are married, please know we are aware some of the dares may not specifically apply to your exact situation. We hope you'll be able to adapt the concepts to your situation with the help of a wiser, older, and local woman friend who has walked in your specific shoes. Know we support and pray for you regardless of your circumstances.

Many of the conversations we will be exploring together apply communication and relationship tools that, if utilized early enough (before the real trouble starts!), can help establish healthier relationships in the long-term. We don't promise a lack of conflict, by any means; all relationships will have conflict. We should neither avoid conflict nor react in damaging ways in the middle of it. We do hope that the areas we cover in the book will help you handle conflict constructively.

Before you get much further, however, you need to understand two things. First, we realize the differences between tweens and teens are innumerable. We also know kids mature at different rates. Because of these variations, we try to avoid discussing specific ages and have included both tween and teen stories. Like having coffee with a more mature mom who has been there, the stories of older kids help prepare us for what could be coming.

Second, this is *not* a how-to-be-an-awesome-parent book. It's also not a book about how to have a perfect, well-adjusted, and well-behaved kid. Your child will hopefully grow and mature from the lessons you learn here, but the purpose of this book is different from many of the excellent parenting books that already exist.

With All Due Respect is a process to help moms connect more deeply with God so that they can create healthier relationships with others. The discipleship method we use is an intense growth experience in a relatively short period of time. This method—adapted from our training courses, Daughters of Sarah® (for wives) and Generations™ (for parents)—is represented here in capsule form.

If you've read my book for married Christian women, *The Respect Dare*, you've already walked through this process in the context of your relationship with your husband. Parenting is another area God uses to help us untangle our identities from the people and things in our lives and focus instead on His opinion of us and our relationship with Him.

If you are a mom who has ever thought to yourself or said to your kid, "Oh no, don't do that. Someone will think X of me!" or felt awesome about yourself and what others think of you because of something your kid has done, this book will help you unhook your identity from your kid's behavior. Gone will be the pressure of performance on both you and your child, and replacing it will be the freedom that comes from understanding who you are in Christ at a deeper level.

Who couldn't use that kind of relief?

On the flip side, this book is not intended to create a hands-off approach to parenting. God told us clearly that the first, most important commandment is to love Him with all our hearts, souls, minds, and strength, and the second is to love others as we love ourselves. If we can help you take a step back from interacting with your kids in unhealthy ways because you are more deeply connected to God, you'll have the space you need to not react to their behavior or your circumstances. Instead, you can seek His wisdom—and then be able to put that wisdom into action without fear, trusting Him for the outcome, regardless of what it is.

As parents we often get stuck in the trap of wanting perfect behavior from our kids, but we need to remember our relationships are with imperfect people—just as we are imperfect—and behavior is often (but not always) the fruit of following God. So what we hope for, instead of perfectly well-behaved kids, are deep relationships, ones where we help our kids mature, walk with them as they clean up mistakes (because they are still going to make them—and what better place than the safety of home to do so!), and learn to love God and others on a deeper level.

The key to these relationships is respect. It may seem

counterintuitive to apply respect to your relationships with your children. Many parents believe that children should respect their parents—and we completely agree—but we also think parents should show respect to their kids. Most parenting experts say that character and behavior are caught by parental example rather than taught by lecture, so we aim for mutually respectful attitudes and behaviors that grow into mutually respectful relationships. This doesn't change your authority as a parent, nor does it diminish the accountability for the family that God holds for you. What respecting your kids can do, however, is reduce long-term negative consequences and create healthy relationships.

If you go through the book and commit to doing the things we ask you to do in the way God leads you to do them (always defer to God instead of to us!), you will grow closer to God and you will likely see your relationships start to change for the better. Yes, you'll learn some conflict-resolution skills. Yes, you'll get ideas from other parents of things that worked for them. More important, though, you will gain a different perspective on how to interact with your kids.

As you read, don't expect each of the stories to connect with your situation perfectly. We are well aware that there are situations we don't address because they are too big for the scope of this book. Drug addiction, sex, pervasive criminal behavior, abuse, mental illness, self-harm, and incest are all significant issues many parents face, and our hearts ache for you if you are dealing with these things. But these bigger issues are things you'll need the help of a licensed counselor to deal with effectively.

Having said all that, however, I think you'll love much of what you read here. The scripturally saturated content will, at the very least, give you the encouragement you need to keep trying. You might even find that some of the tools you need for dealing with the bigger issues are actually demonstrated in our discussion of the smaller ones.

Most of all, remember this: even God Himself had kids who didn't obey and were not perfect! I don't know about you, but Adam and Eve help me grab a comforting perspective about this entire parenting gig. I hope thinking about His children and their responses to Him lets you give yourself a break in the self-criticism department! My bottom-line encouragement for you is simply this: pray and don't quit. All the struggles are a part of the journey, both our children's and ours. Scripture says, "Train up a child in the way he should go, and *when he is old he will not depart from it*" (Prov. 22:6 NKJV, emphasis added). *Old* in my world means the jury is out for a while—at least until these kids are in their late seventies!

LOVE TO YOU,

Nina Roesner

A Note from Debbie . . .

In 2006, I was at the end of my rope with one of my teenage children. I had spent the previous few years reading every book on parenting, reading Scripture, attending seminars, and doing research, as well as seeking assistance from Christian counselors, in an attempt to resolve the conflict that always seemed to reside in our home. Friends and family all offered advice, but they had different perspectives on what was best and nothing seemed to work. My husband and I were like deer in headlights, afraid to make a move, fearful of the future. Finally, after months of prayer and counseling, we made the most difficult decision we had ever made in our lives: we removed one of our children from our home for a short period of time.

Our desire was emotional healing for our family. We thought this time and distance would give us rest from the war that seemed to be taking place under our roof. Instead, this became a time of work; in fact, it was the hardest work I had ever encountered. As weekly counseling sessions unfolded via telephone, with my husband and me on one end and our teen and counselor on the other, I began to realize how my words became more measured as I responded to my child. Because my goal was emotional healing, I chose words that conveyed understanding and openness to ideas other than my own in order to convey respect, agreement, trust, and love. It was amazing how the shift in perspective toward an emotional healthy relationship brought change to the outcome of a conversation.

The situation we were in was not just about this child but also very much about us. The only way we could make a difference was to work toward the goal of successfully launching our child into the world, letting the natural consequences of life be the teacher, rather than emotionally reacting to each individual situation we encountered.

At the same time, a course was being offered at our local church called Daughters of Sarah®. Friends who had already taken the course were talking about how it had revolutionized their marriages. With all that my husband and I had endured over the past several years, I felt like our relationship was stronger than ever. I didn't think I needed the course, but as a former corporate trainer, I was especially drawn to the comments being made: "I've never had training like this before," and "I am such a different person," and "I liked the accountability and how every time we met was a new and different learning opportunity." It piqued my interest, and I eventually enrolled, a decision that truly changed my life.

Daughters of Sarah® was about examining my life, my experiences, and my reactions. The reading and homework assignments forced me to try new behaviors, which I started applying in all my relationships in our home—with my tween, two teens, and twenty-something. I didn't know it at the time, but the reason the course had such a huge impact was because the training method was steeped in

Scripture, and when combined with the power of the Holy Spirit, I watched myself and the other women around me be dramatically changed. Dealing with conflict and fostering healthy relationships became easier for us all.

Shortly thereafter I started getting phone calls from parents who were in trouble. The fact that my husband and I had previously taken dramatic steps with our teen could hardly go unnoticed, and I found myself walking beside other parents who were hurting. Their situations were sometimes significantly different, but the skills I had learned still applied. God used these brave souls and the privilege of helping them to also bring me healing, to give me confidence in what I had learned, and to show me that I was not the only mother dealing with tough situations.

In 2011, with the help of Nina Roesner, who authored Daughters of Sarah®, I designed a course for parents called Generations™. My husband and several pastors also offered their wisdom to help me capture how parenting roles play out differently for men and women. The goal was to help parents catch the essence of their God-ordained purpose in parenting—*to launch their children into the world*!

I've been privileged through the years—having experienced the transformation in my own family's relationships and having watched God do a mighty work in other families—to witness the change that can happen when parents actively choose to be relationship architects in their homes. As a facilitator of both Daughters of Sarah® and Generations™, and through my experience as a family relationship coach, I have seen hundreds of people positively impacted by the biblical concept of respect, and this book brings those principles taught in those courses to the wider world.

While this book does not capture the full experience of all that occurs when one goes through the entire course of Generations™, it will help you lay a foundation and assess your implementation of biblical principles with your children. I believe and pray that it will help parents continue to build or even *rebuild* relationships with their children, no matter what stage of life they might be in.

With All Due Respect is a book of dares for us as moms. While you can do this book alone, we encourage you to do it in a group with other women to get the full impact of the experience. You can also sign up for our e-course and do it with women from around the world from the comfort of your home.

Many have asked me about the dad element, and by all means, we encourage your husbands to be part of this journey with you. While the questions in this book are specifically tailored to moms, we have dad-specific questions available as a download on the ministry website at www.greaterimpact.org. We intend to include them in the small group guide as well.

As mothers, we must actively choose to let go of control, calm our fears, and bravely release our children into the unfamiliar, trusting that God has a plan for each step our children take. We have the opportunity to dare to dream, dare to hope, dare to no longer wrap our self-esteem up in these wonderful but sinful children whom God has given us on loan. This book will dare you to obey His Word and to let go of the habits that so often lead us to the destruction of relationships. We dare you to take your sense of self from God's perspective, trusting Him when you have no knowledge of what the future holds, and to risk being personally changed in order to positively affect all your family relationships.

It is my hope and prayer that by reading and actively participating in *With All Due Respect*, you will experience God on a deeper level. I love how Gary Thomas says in his book *Sacred Parenting*, "Raising children shapes our souls." May this book provide the impetus to launch your children without fear, while you learn how to rest in the assurance that God is ultimately the One in control.

"LET GO . . . AND LET GOD,"

Debbie

DEAL WITH THESE FIRST
Expectations

You are reading this book because you have children who are teens or tweens. Your desire is to improve your relationship with your child in a way that honors and glorifies God. You might be desperate to begin the journey, holding this book in your hand as a last-ditch effort to hope for a future with your child. Or perhaps you are not sure if you really need this book. Maybe you look at some of your friends and their children, and you know your relationship with your kid could be a lot worse. Even if the relationship with your child is good, though, remember you can always make any relationship better.

If we asked you right now to think of one small, tangible thing that would show you that you are making progress in how you behave with your child, what would you say? Notice we didn't ask you to think of a small, tangible thing you would like to be different in your child's behavior. We want you to focus on something that would be different in your behavior as you interact with your child.

Typically, our expectations are things we want our children to do, dreams we have of what they will accomplish in life and who they will be as people, behaviors we want to see them exhibit, especially in front of our friends. Those expectations fall in the "do" and "don't" columns of things that will make us smile or things that could potentially embarrass us. But often we forget about setting expectations for ourselves as parents. We nag, demand, and impose rules on our children, hoping to see change, only to find ourselves caught up in the same cycle of disappointment and fear that our dreams for our kids will never materialize. What we sometimes forget—or perhaps haven't yet realized—is that we can break out of that cycle if we are willing to let go of our expectations for our kids and instead choose to set new expectations for ourselves.

When we refer to the concept of expectations in this book, we recognize that we are addressing both positive and negative aspects of the word. It is unhealthy to set ourselves up for disappointment by expecting our children to fulfill unrealized dreams of ours. It is healthy, on the other hand, for us to expect *ourselves* to behave in certain ways to be more successful in connecting with our children. While most parents desire positive behavior from their children, good behavior may be all they are getting without the understanding and foundation to create lasting change. In the end, it must originate in the heart, and the thing that transforms the heart is relationship. That's why we encourage you to look at the expectations you have for yourself in building relationship.

An expectation you might write for yourself could look something like this: "I will no longer raise my voice when I see (insert your child's name) leave his bike outside after dark." Or, "I will be calm when I see my daughter speed into the driveway." Maybe it should be something like, "I will no longer make snide comments about (insert your child's name)'s new haircut, even though I find it appalling," or even, "I'll actively choose to gently engage in conflict instead of acting angry or avoidant when issues need to be addressed."

As parents, we need to stop clinging to our own expectations of our children. Yes, we can set the stage for what God would desire of our child, but ultimately, our child's decisions are just that: their decisions. Remember, the end-goal is relationship, to love our child unconditionally and emerge as a coach in his or her life.

Take a few minutes, and ask God to reveal three tangible

outcomes that would indicate progress is being made *by you* to let go of old expectations, release control, and set new, healthier ones. Remember, your behavior is the only thing you can definitively influence and control. Make sure these statements are measurable so that when you review the list in the future, you will know that things are different. These are areas you are going to focus on while you are on this journey. A page in your journal might look something like this:

EXPECTATIONS FOR MY PROGRESS AS MEREDITH'S PARENT

1. I will find a way to connect with Meredith at least once a day for a minimum of fifteen minutes doing something that we both enjoy—going for a walk, scrapbooking, watching a movie, shopping, or just having hot chocolate.
2. I will refrain from saying anything to Meredith about the way she dresses, even though I do not approve of the amount of skin she shows. She knows how I feel and my lectures are falling on deaf ears anyway, so I am choosing to stop the battle that I typically start.
3. I will choose not to engage in conflict when Meredith comes in after curfew. I will simply turn out the lights, tell her good night, and talk to her the next morning, beginning in a gentle way, when we've both had some sleep.

For parents with more than one child in this age category, we would encourage you to focus on one kid at a time. Experience has shown that when you choose to concentrate specifically on interactions within the most difficult parent/child relationship first, you will have new skills to help you eventually build relationship with each of the other children as they start taking notice of the changes happening with the first. Don't place too many expectations on yourself. Remember, we are taking baby steps.

On a separate sheet of paper, under the heading "Expectations of (your child's name) That I Release to God," write three tangible, measurable statements, similar to those above, that you have held for this child. These might be unrealized dreams of yours for your child or possibly something you desire that is outside your child's interest, gifting, or God's plan. An example might be your desire for your son to attend your alma mater and enter the same field that you did. These expectations that we are releasing could also be unrealistic demands on behavior; for example, you wanting your daughter's room to be immaculate every time you walk into it.

Do not share these expectations with your child or your spouse, but instead, take this second piece of paper and place it in an envelope. After sealing the envelope, put a date exactly six months from now on the front. Clip the envelope to your calendar or put the envelope in a place where you will be able to find it later. Then mark your calendar with the date you will be opening the document. Resist the temptation to think about it or open it in advance. Just continue moving forward in your learning and application of respect for the next several weeks. At the end of the six-month period, we encourage you to open your envelope and go to our website (http://www.greaterimpact.org/respect-dare/the-envelope/). There you will receive further instructions on what to do with the list you wrote.

In the meantime, we want to encourage you to talk about the expectations you have set for yourself with your child's father. Having accountability with him in your parenting pursuits will move both of you forward in your relationship. Encourage him to change some behaviors as he sees the impact your changes are making, but resist the urge to verbally correct him when he makes mistakes. With a gentle and quiet spirit, encourage each other to do things differently next time. We're all human, and sometimes we need to remember the old saying, "Whatever is worth doing right is worth doing poorly until we get it right." Frequently read over the list of personal expectations you wrote in your journal.

Remember, too, not to set expectations of your children's father. This is a separate journey for each of you in the parenting process. That means each of you might be progressing at different rates. Don't get caught up in the "I'm a better parent than you are" game, but rejoice together that your child is at least in relationship with one of you, if that is your situation. Realize as well that this expectation animal will rear its ugly head multiple times, so don't get discouraged if you have to combat this regularly.

Whether you are part of a divorced family, blended family, single-parent family, or an intact family, remember that each situation has its own set of unique circumstances. God can bring healing to any relationship if we are willing to look deep within ourselves to see where He wants us to grow.

Pray with us as we begin this journey together:

Father in heaven,

I am Your precious child. You understand more than I ever could the pain of not being in full relationship with Your children. Just like I fail to reach out to You who gave me life and to heed Your instruction, I see my child doing the same. I have so many hopes and dreams for (your child's name), just as I am sure You have for me.

God, be merciful to me and hear my prayer as I lay my requests before You and wait in expectation. There are times I am worn out from groaning; all night long I flood my bed with weeping and drench my couch with tears over things my child has done. My soul finds rest only in You. Your Word tells me that You will give me strength when I am weary from the battles of parenting. Lord, You alone give me hope. Help me run this race and not grow weary.

Sometimes I am so determined to try to correct the things my child does that are wrong that I forget to offer encouragement. I also forget to guard my own heart in the journey to parent more like You. Help me, Lord, see what is true about my child. Help me see the good, the things he does right. Help me learn that what I pay attention to will grow.

You have me at this place, on this journey with my child, Lord, to change me. Help me look to You for wisdom. Draw me closer to You in ways I never dreamed possible so that fear will not overtake me. I know I cannot change on my own, but with You all things are possible.

Lord, I want to be the best parent You made me to be. I desire relationship with (your child's name) that bears fruit for generations to come. May my efforts be pleasing in Your sight.

In Jesus' name,
Amen.

ASSESS YOUR PARENTING
INTERACTIONS

Jesus answered and said to him, "If anyone loves Me, he will keep My
word; and My Father will love him, and We will come to him and
make Our home with him. He who does not love Me does not keep My
words; and the word which you hear is not Mine but the Father's who
sent Me."

—JOHN 14:23–24 NKJV

L et's begin by assessing your current interactions with your child
using a tool that addresses what it means to be a biblical parent.
Remember that each of us is created differently, and each of our kids
has different needs and bents. What works in one home may not
work in another. What works for dad might not work for mom. God
gave your child two parents who each think and operate differently,
so we encourage you to think about how you operate in concert with
one another. You each should have separate relationships with your
child, as well as the relationship you call family.

If you are a single mom or your husband is not fully engaged
in your family life, take heart. God Himself will walk beside you
in the process of parenting, just as He does in two-parent families.
Of course, you may have to work at things a little harder as the
struggles become more intense through the teen years. We would
encourage you to find other adults who might be willing to walk
alongside your child to offer the balance and support that you alone
can't provide. Above all, depend on Him to supply your needs.

If you are part of a blended or divorced situation, we would encourage you to seek God's wisdom as to whether you should include the divorced parent or how to incorporate the step-parent into this process. God knows the struggles you face. He'll provide a way, as He loves your child deeply.

Be assured that this book does not prescribe a one-size-fits-all mentality when it comes to parenting. None of us was created to be supermom. Our desire is to help each of us be aware of some of the important aspects of parenting that sometimes fall off the radar screen during the busyness of life.

You will see as you go through the Personal Parenting Assessment below that generalized terms are used rather than specific ones to allow for the different experiences that you may have. Please note that the words *teen* or *tween* show up interchangeably, since the questions apply to both age categories. You'll also see that the assessment addresses habits and attitudes that the Bible encourages us to practice as parents. Prayerfully consider each of the issues in the assessment as an opportunity for your own personal development. As we allow God to search our hearts and examine our minds in our desire to love our children as the Lord loves us, may He give us wisdom, knowledge, and understanding.

Personal Parenting Assessment

DISCIPLE

- Do I spend consistent time in prayer daily?
- Do I read the Bible frequently?
- Do I daily make decisions based on what I think would please God?
- Is my heart filled with gratitude for all God has done for me?

- Do I choose to live my life for God more than I am concerned about what other people think?
- Do I understand my need for the Holy Spirit living within me, guiding my steps, instead of depending on my own abilities?
- Is my relationship with God a living experience more than an intellectual concept?
- Do I regularly attend church?

DISCIPLER

- Am I more concerned with being holy or making my teen happy?
- Do I actively discuss spiritual things with my teen?
- Do I help my teen navigate difficulties by going to the Bible?
- Do I let my teen know what I am struggling with (appropriately) and ask for prayer?
- Do I apologize and seek forgiveness from my teen when I hurt him or her or am wrong?
- Do I pray with my teen on a regular basis?

COMMUNICATOR

- Am I concise in my communication more than I ramble and go off on tangents?
- Am I considered a good listener?
- Do I handle conflict with a gentle and calm tone more than being emotional?
- Does my teen confide in me?
- Do I communicate positively more than I am critical or sarcastic?
- Do I know the difference between criticism and coaching?
- Do I encourage and support more than I criticize and correct my kids in public?

- Do I only share stories about my kid with his or her permission?
- Do I have emotional control more than I react or judge when my teen opens up to me?
- Do I daily point out things my kid has done well?
- Does my teen perceive me as a positive person more than a complainer?
- Do I seek feedback from my kids about my attitude toward them?
- Do I know how to give advice to my teens in a way that allows them to hear it and do they often take it?
- Does my teen seek me out for advice?
- Do I communicate openly with my teens more than I give them ultimatums?

CONFIDENT AND ASSURED PARENT

- Do others perceive me as confident and God-dependent rather than arrogant, aggressive, controlling, manipulative, timid, or fearful?
- Do I feel courageous enough to do what God wants me to do?
- Do I have a spirit of power, love, and self-discipline?
- Do I know God's purposes for my life and trust He will help me succeed?
- Do I engage in difficult discussions in a healthy way, or do I avoid them or handle them aggressively?
- Am I confident in the decisions I make as a parent?
- Do I know when and how to let my teen fail and when and how to step in to help?
- Am I confident that God has things under control, so I have no need to manipulate others to make things happen a certain way?
- Do I apologize to my family members, including my kids,

without making excuses or blaming someone else when I make mistakes?

- Am I preparing to launch my kid into adulthood more than trying to control his or her behavior?
- Can I receive criticism, praise, and negative or positive feedback about my tween or teen without taking it personally?
- Do my family members trust me?

FAMILY RELATIONSHIP ARCHITECT

- Am I connected to my kid's other parent in a healthy relationship?
- Do I openly discuss concerns for our kids with the goal of reaching a unified decision with the other parent?
- Do I have peace more than I struggle with a blended family where relationships aren't clearly defined?
- Do I suggest ways to engage our kid in a deeper relationship with both parents separately and together?
- Do I understand and actively model healthy relationships with family members?
- Do I pursue learning the desires of each family member and encourage support by other family members?
- Do I encourage healthy communication with extended family either by providing opportunities or solidifying the boundaries?

What About You?

- ☐ What feelings or thoughts emerged from doing the evaluation?
- ☐ What do you think might have triggered the emotion or thought?

☐ Can those feelings and thoughts be trusted? Why or why not?

☐ Choose two areas that you feel most led to work on at this time. Why those?

☐ What would happen if you were able to grow significantly in those two areas in the next forty days?

☐ What would that mean for you, your tween or teen, and the other parent?

☐ Take some time to pray and ask God to give you clear insight regarding how things would be different if you were able to make changes in the areas you would like to grow in from the assessment. God desires to strengthen us to be the best parents we can be. Invite Him to walk beside you on this journey, revealing ways in which you can grow and be better equipped to handle the trials that come in the parenting process.

Pray with us:

Lord, I confess I don't know which way to turn half the time. I have trouble discerning Your will in the middle of the average day. I ache to have healthy relationships with the members of my family, to bring glory to You this way. I also confess I am often more concerned about things working out the way I deem is "good" than I am with what You might have in mind. I try to control. I don't know You well enough to only care about what You want. I want more peace and less angst in our family. Help me be a peacemaker; help me be courageous enough to follow You. Fill me with Your Spirit.

Help me disciple my kids well, and, Lord, may they know You. Bring them into relationship with You, O God. Thank

You for Jesus. I fully know You are also a parent. You know and understand sacrificial love better than any of us, so remind me of that. Remind me that You love my kids more than their dad and I ever could. Help me trust You in that.

It's in Jesus' name, I pray.

Amen.

Dare 2 REVISIT YOUR CHILDHOOD

Consider it pure joy, my brothers and sisters, whenever you face trials of many kinds, because you know that the testing of your faith produces perseverance. Let perseverance finish its work so that you may be mature and complete, not lacking anything. If any of you lacks wisdom, you should ask God, who gives generously to all without finding fault, and it will be given to you.

—James 1:2–5

Tracy stood outside the van wishing life were different. She was tired of the same race week after week.

"Tyler, you are going to make Jonathan late for practice! Junior high basketball is different. The coach expects us to be on time or Jonathan won't be able to start in Saturday's game. Get in the car right now!"

"But, Mom, I wanted to get my cars," six-year-old Tyler whined as he tried to open the van door with a juice box in one hand and his dinner bag in another. Reaching down for his case of cars, he accidentally spilled his juice on the carpet of the van.

"Tyler, look what you've done!" Tracy yelled. "Your dad just cleaned this van, and now you've ruined the carpet. I'll never get that red stain out. You knew we had to leave! Get in here right now, and get that seat belt on! You are making Jonathan late!"

A family sit-down dinner in the evenings seemed to be a thing of the past. Tonight Mark was picking up Lindsay from her swim practice after he finished his workout at the gym. Tomorrow night

Tracy had to run to the grocery store and do the swim carpool while Mark got Tyler to tae kwon do and picked up Jonathan from his basketball practice. Sometimes the weekends were even worse with all-day swim meets that seemed to last forever!

Dropping into bed that night, Tracy leaned over to kiss Mark good night. As she laid her head on her pillow, she voiced her thoughts. "Why do we do this to ourselves? All this running seems to be a waste at times. It seemed as though every time I turned around tonight I was yelling at Tyler. Some mom I am."

Mark tried to console her before they both fell asleep exhausted.

Tracy called Mark the next day at work to see if they could spend some time together without the kids after Saturday's swim meet. "I think we need to talk about the treadmill we are on as a family. How do we get off? Do some thinking and praying about it, okay?"

Over a quiet dinner that Saturday, Tracy and Mark talked about the way things were and each of their concerns. They looked at all the positives as well as the downsides of the family life they had created.

"You know, Mark," Tracy ventured, "I may have figured out why we do this to ourselves. When I was a kid, I wasn't allowed to do any sports. My brothers played everything they wanted to, and it wasn't fair that I had to sit at home while they were out having fun. I always said that all my kids would be allowed to do the activities I wasn't allowed to do when I was a kid." She paused thoughtfully, then continued, "I remember you saying once that your dad made you quit every sports team you played on because something would make him mad. Is that right?"

"Yeah . . ."

"Maybe that's it. Maybe we've allowed our kids to do whatever activity they want to do because we didn't get to as kids. Subconsciously, we're trying to right the wrongs we think our parents did to us."

"Wow, I never thought about that. You might be right. Maybe we need to start thinking a little more about the legacy we want to leave to our kids and grandkids."

> Bottom line: If we take a second look at our own childhood, we can learn a lot about our current parenting.

We are all affected by our childhoods through the legacy handed down from our parents. The opportunities we were never given or the pain we were forced to endure can cloud our judgment. Even if we think we grew up in ideal circumstances, once we reach the stressful years of parenting, we sometimes find ourselves rethinking those idyllic childhood memories as reality starts to show up in our own parenting. Things we vowed we'd never say or do become things that haunt us, or we choose to ignore problematic behaviors from our children in fear that we will become just like our parents.

However, maturity and wisdom will flood into our parenting if we are willing to sift through the past honestly, discarding the unhealthy while finding and implementing that which is based on solid biblical principles. Doing this simple activity will shine light onto some of the lies we have believed that have become filters through which we see our current situation. The awareness that comes from this will provide the opportunity to do things differently. Sorting through the past can take a long time, but the habits we foster as we choose to learn from it can positively impact our own children and the generations to come.

What About You?

☐ Take time today to ask God to bring an experience to your mind that has impacted a choice you've made in your parenting. Who was there? When was this incident? Where were you? How old were you? What happened? If this is something that happened many times, just pick one particular occasion and describe it as best as you can. Do it in a way that allows you to relive that moment.

☐ What possible reactions do you have in your current parenting because of that one event? For example, in Tracy and Mark's story, Mark might react to his father's previous actions today by thinking, *I can never speak to a coach about my son because I'll end up getting mad and I don't want to put him in a position to have to quit a team.* If you were Tracy, your takeaway from your childhood could be, *I was a girl who couldn't do anything outside the home, so I'm going to make sure my daughter gets every opportunity she wants no matter what the sacrifice.* Set a timer for seven minutes, and make a list of all the reactions you may have due to that incident.

☐ Write a prayer of release for yourself in your journal, letting go of your natural reactions to your circumstances and asking God to take away any unhealthy thinking you've developed. Ask Him to renew those thoughts with truth.

Pray with us:

Lord, it doesn't matter if my childhood holds fond memories or is riddled with pain. You allowed the past to be part of who I am. Help me make sense of the road I've been down and the childhood experiences that have colored my thinking about how I am to behave as a parent.

Father, I ask that You bring a specific incident to my mind from my childhood that has taught me about parenting. Whether good or bad, it doesn't matter. I want to understand the truth about the childhood I experienced so that I can be the parent You desire me to be. Show me any lies I have come to believe as a result of this incident. Reveal to me how this one incident impacts how I currently interact with my kids.

Oh, how I desire wisdom as I go through the ups and downs of parenting. Teach me Your truths, and release me from the falsehoods I've come to believe throughout my life. Help me parent through the lens of the Holy Spirit.

In the precious name of Jesus,
Amen.

Dare 3 # FOCUS ON GOD'S VISION

"For I know the plans I have for you," declares the LORD, *"plans to prosper you and not to harm you, plans to give you hope and a future."*
—JEREMIAH 29:11

Train up a child in the way he should go: and when he is old, he shall not depart from it.
—PROVERBS 22:6 KJV

One of the most difficult things about parenting is letting go of the expectations we have for our children. We often come into parenting with a ton of baggage, wanting to parent the same way we've been parented or wanting to avoid a number of aspects from our own childhood experiences. Sometimes we wrap our identities up in our kids' behaviors and their achievements, or lack thereof. We worry about what other people think of us instead of realizing our children are not really ours, that they belong to God.

The phrase "train up a child in the way he should go" from Proverbs 22:6 (NKJV) literally means "teach him according to his palette." This means we need to get to know our kids deeply and understand how God created them, *then* do our best to facilitate growth in the ways God created them, instead of focusing on what we want or think they should be.

This is not an easy task or perspective to continually hold.

It's incredibly important, however, if we want to do what is right in God's sight to develop the people He has trusted into our care. We should not take this responsibility lightly. Equally important is realizing God has a vision for us too, and our parenting is a context through which He will grow us. Desiring to grow in our parenting brings glory to God and helps our relationships with our kids.

Bottom line: By actively choosing to grow toward the vision God has for us as parents, we assist God in the vision He has for our kids.

What About You?

☐ Using the assessment you did in Dare 1, write a positive purpose statement in the present tense, describing the kind of parent you deeply desire to be in four months and how you will get there.

Keep your statements positive, avoiding the "I'm no longer," "I'm not," or "I don't" statements. Write what you will do instead that is positive, and use "I am" language, as opposed to "I want to be" or "I will." Note the tense is present, as if it were already a reality. In about two hundred words, be as descriptive as possible. Here is an example:

I am a faith-filled parent, spending time with God daily in prayer and listening to Him. I read His Word every day and do my best to apply it. I ask Him for advice in the middle of moments with my kids. I treat everyone in my family with respect, knowing that this is how God wants me to treat those He created and loves. I ask questions before firing off lectures. I consult my tweens and teens before making decisions that affect them. I am interested in each of my kids and spend time talking with them about their world and what is important to them. I regularly apologize when I hurt their feelings. I make hard decisions about privileges but also work on the relationship so that the rules don't end up in rebellion. I encourage my kids to do the things they are interested in. I remain calm when they drop crazy ideas in my lap. I have a peace about me that provides comfort and a sense of security to my family. I remember that my identity is not wrapped up in what my kids or my friends think of me, but rather what God thinks of me. I do my best to provide a united front with their father and encourage a good relationship with him. I ask them without nagging about their relationships with God and others.

- When you have finished writing your vision statement, rewrite it as a prayer, tape it somewhere you will see it daily, and begin to act each day as if you were already this person. Continue to pray this prayer and act "as if" moment to moment, starting over when (not if, but when!) you fail as you work your way through the rest of this book.

Pray with us:

Lord, I want to be the best that I can be for You and for my family. Sometimes it is so easy to want to change the things I see in my children, but I don't take the time to pause and question what they see in me—what I am modeling for them. I'm so glad I have this opportunity to look into the future at who I can become if I spend time in Your Word and with You in prayer. Bring an awareness to my thoughts when I make mistakes in my daily interactions with my kids, prompting me to apologize or seek clarification. Help me not to justify my actions but to humbly admit that the behavior I might display to my children is not bringing glory to You or teaching my children the behaviors I want them to catch. Create in me a desire to grow to be more like You with both grace and humility.

In Jesus' name,
Amen.

Dare 4   PUSH THE RESET BUTTON

Do not be deceived: God cannot be mocked. A man reaps what he sows.
—GALATIANS 6:7

I can't believe we did it again! How does that kid always out-smart us?"

Dianne and Derrick thought they had come up with the perfect consequence for their daughter's new attempts at testing the curfew limits they had put into place. If Kari came home late, she wouldn't be allowed to drive to school the next day. Second missed curfew: two days. If Kari hit number three, she'd lose the car for a week.

It had seemed like a fair way to solve the problem. Both Dianne and Derrick had felt confident that it would work, especially since Kari liked her newfound independence with her driver's license and hated riding the school bus.

It wasn't like they were over-the-top strict. Dianne had talked to several other parents with kids similar in age to Kari. The curfews in their homes fell right in line with what they had set for Kari.

Adding to the problem was that on the weekends, Dianne and Derrick were exhausted. Waiting up to see if Kari arrived home on time was keeping them from getting much needed sleep, not to mention the fact that arguments usually ensued when Kari got back, keeping everyone up even later.

"Kari seems to be one of those kids who thinks the rules don't apply to her," Dianne lamented.

The first time Kari missed curfew after the new rules were in place, she'd pointed out that Dianne had an appointment that would take her by the school the next morning. "Mom, can you just drop me off?"

She had asked politely, so Dianne decided to give her a break from the bus. *After all, I am going right past the school*, she rationalized. *I'd rather do that than have to wait to make sure she gets on the bus.*

The second time Kari missed curfew, she rode the bus the first day as planned, but then day number two went south. Kari didn't manage her time and missed the bus. "Mom, I have a chemistry test today! If I miss, Mr. Robinson will make me take the more difficult test tomorrow. I can't bomb this test or I'll get a C in chemistry this semester. You don't want me to do that, do you?"

With that last plea, Dianne found herself fishing in the hall closet for a jacket and her keys.

When Kari pushed the curfew limit for the third time, the same game played out. As fate would have it, Dianne's four-year-old was running a fever, and she had spent most of the night rocking her son. She wasn't even dressed when Kari missed the bus yet again.

"Mom, I have to be there. Our group is presenting our project in English. I have all the props."

Exhaustion took over. Dianne's defenses were down. "Go ahead and take the car. We'll decide how to handle it later," she wearily responded.

The next day Dianne shared her tale of woe with her best friend, Charlotte. Thankfully, Charlotte was a little further down the parenting road than Dianne was, as she had college-aged kids and one teen still at home.

"What about putting an alarm at the top of the stairs by your room that Kari has to shut off when she gets home to help solve the sleep problem?" Charlotte suggested. "A different consequence that doesn't require your involvement might also be in order."

Dianne thought this was a great idea and discussed it with her husband. They decided to give it a try, along with a new plan for consequences.

"Kari," Derrick began the conversation. "Your mom and I are concerned about you repeatedly missing curfew. We put a consequence in place that didn't tie directly to the offense, and you've put your mom in a situation of bailing you out. Obviously we didn't think that through very well, so we have a new plan. As I have mentioned before, being on time is an important skill in adulthood. It affects almost every area of our lives. I want to provide opportunities for you to learn this while you are in our home so this isn't a problem for you later in the adult world. So here's what your mom and I want to do."

He took a breath.

"Your mom and I are no longer going to wait up for you. We're going to bed. There will be an alarm at the top of the stairs by our bedroom door for you to turn off when you come in. If you're late, the alarm will wake us up, and we'll know you aren't home. If that happens, you will need to be home one hour earlier the next time you go out. If you miss a second time, you will not be able to go out at night on the following weekend. You have a lot of talent, Kari, and I hope you'll be successful in the future. This will help you work on the punctuality skills you'll need in order to be successful in life."

The new consequences worked great. Dianne realized she was blessed to have women friends to connect with and garner pearls of wisdom from. She also realized she needed to think more carefully about how to approach consequences for her children.

Bottom line: When consequences fail, push the reset button and work out a better solution.

As parents, our desire should be to watch consequences flow naturally (either good or bad) from our child's behavior. If we need to restructure the consequences we've already put into place, it should ideally be done in a way that helps the teen understand that it's for the purpose of working toward a healthy life balance. Through the process, our child should feel our respect and desire to help them grow.

What About You?

☐ What are three recent disciplinary actions you've taken with your kids? Are they punishments (where we want them to suffer until they make the right choice) or consequences that will help them grow as a result?

☐ Have any of those consequences negatively impacted you or your spouse? If so, how?

☐ How have you involved your tween or teen in a discussion about behaviors and what would be reasonable as discipline *before* the action requiring consequences takes place? If you haven't, schedule a time for this discussion. Talk through issues, and land on a naturally related consequence that impacts only your tween or teen. Be sure to write it down so that you can refer back to it if there is a question about what was agreed upon.

☐ Do you regularly get advice from other godly parents further down the parenting road than you? If not, is there someone you admire as a parent whom you can ask for help? Remember, they don't have to have perfect kids, but they do need to be godly people who are humble and transparent.

Pray with us:

Dear heavenly Father,

Regardless of whether I am in the valley or on the mountaintop with my children, I want to enter Your gates with thanksgiving and Your courts with praise about the opportunities that refine me and help grow my children. You gave me Scripture as an instruction book, but it doesn't tell me exactly what to do in every situation that I encounter with my children. You know that sometimes what I think is right as a consequence for my child isn't the right thing to do at all. Help me, just as You did when Solomon prayed in 2 Chronicles, "Give me wisdom and knowledge, that I may lead this people."[1] You have entrusted these children to me. My heart's cry is that You will help me be a good mother to them.

Lord, I pray that my first instinct will be to go to You for wisdom when I am struggling as a parent. But even so, would You also bring into my life a godly woman who is further on the journey than I? Someone I can feel free to share my shortcomings with as a parent? My prayer is that this woman will be willing to be real about what worked and didn't work with her own kids so that I won't make similar mistakes. Lord, while I know she won't have all Your wisdom, may she at least be a woman with perspective.

Give me a spirit of discernment in how I should handle each situation with my child. When I interact with my child in a way that doesn't go well, give me the wisdom to reset the consequence, rather than give up and let things slide. Help me tenaciously persevere in building a relationship that will last over a lifetime.

In Jesus' name,
Amen.

 *Dare 5* ## BE CAREFUL WITH YOUR WORDS

"But what comes out of the mouth proceeds from the heart, and this defiles a person. For out of the heart come evil thoughts, murder, adultery, sexual immorality, theft, false witness, slander."
—MATTHEW 15:18–19 ESV

Sharise walked into the hallway and said to her daughter, Amanda, "Baby, you'll need to do the stairs. There's dog hair on them."

This was after Amanda had already put the vacuum away, thinking she was done with her daily chore. Sharise expected to hear, "I know!" escape from her daughter's lips. Maybe she'd get a complimentary eye-roll too.

But the words that came forth from Amanda's lips completely surprised and delighted her mom. "You are so right!"

Sharise smiled. Several days before, she and Amanda had discussed the use of the phrase "I know." Sharise had explained to her tween that she had caught herself being disrespectful to her daughter by using that phrase when Amanda reminded her of an upcoming event that she needed Sharise to drive her to. She admitted she should have said, "You are right!" instead of quipping, "I know!" and then apologized for being snarky to her daughter, promising to try to communicate more respectfully in the future. She explained to Amanda that she had not treated her as if she was precious to her or to God and that she had confessed and asked God to forgive her as well.

In that moment, Sharise put a little dare together for both of them. "I know I've modeled the wrong thing for you, Amanda, but I'd like you to know you do this too. I'm guessing we both know how it makes us feel. I need to work on this one, and so do you. Want to do it together?"

Amanda smiled. "I think you're right, Mom," she replied. "I would like to work on this with you."

> Bottom line: Ditch the sarcasm. Your kids will feel more respected, and in turn they'll treat you with more respect.

We often focus on getting and sometimes demanding respect from our children. But how often do we examine our own behavior to determine whether we are treating our children with respect? Just as with every other aspect of parenting, kids model what they see. Sometimes it's the simple phrases or the small actions that speak the loudest. Ask God to help you be more respectful to your kids. Say, "You are right!" instead of, "I know!" and admit your own mistakes.

The good news is that a change in behavior often leads to a change in the heart, and it usually works the other way around too. If you are choosing to follow Christ, He'll transform your heart.

What About You?

☐ Think of the last time your tween or teen exasperated you over a small thing. How did you respond? If you did not respond gently, confess your sin to God and ask for forgiveness. Know He has forgiven you, and receive that forgiveness.

☐ How freely do you admit when you are wrong? How does this humble attitude model respect for your child?

☐ How does the thought of admitting wrongdoing or fault to your child make you feel? Ask God to reveal any issues with a desire to control, pride, or fear to you, and ask Him to grow you in these areas.

☐ Apologize to your child for the way you have treated her, and be specific. Promise to try to do better (and then do so!), and ask her to forgive you. If it is a deeply ingrained habit, you might even consider being vulnerable enough to ask your child to help you grow in this area by saying, "Ouch!" when you respond this way to her.

☐ Are your responses to your child ones that indicate arrogance? How often are you sarcastic or prideful in your responses? Instead of retorting with sarcasm or an "I know!" say, "You are right."

Pray with us:

Lord, I know I bring habits into my home that are not pleasing in Your sight. Most of the time I am blind to them. Open my eyes so that I might see the good and want to model positive interactions with my children. Sometimes the little things might not seem like a big deal; however, I want to create an environment in my home where my children know I value them. I want to create a warm place where they have hope that they are doing things right, so they see it as a refuge against the negative they face on a daily basis when they are at school or with their friends.

Give me wisdom in picking areas where my children can help me grow. Help me be vulnerable enough with my children that I will allow them to honestly give me feedback so I can become more like You. Help me take brave steps when I'm feeling vulnerable, especially if I'm afraid of losing control or worried my kids will think I don't have all the answers. The truth is, I don't! Help me remember that when I admit to not being perfect, I am speaking truth into a situation and giving them permission to do the same thing. Thank You, Father, for giving me these children to grow me.

In Your precious Son's name,
Amen.

 **Dare 6** # COMMUNICATE RESPECT EARLY

Fathers, do not provoke your children to anger by the way you treat them. Rather, bring them up with the discipline and instruction that comes from the Lord.

—Ephesians 6:4 nlt

Fathers, do not provoke or irritate or exasperate your children [with demands that are trivial or unreasonable or humiliating or abusive; nor by favoritism or indifference; treat them tenderly with lovingkindness], so that they will not lose heart and become discouraged or unmotivated [with their spirits broken].

—Colossians 3:21 amp

He's making me crazy!" Carol threw up her hands and whined to her husband.

"He feels the same way about you," Dale responded.

"I know—and I don't know what to do."

"He's becoming a man."

"What? He's twelve!"

"I know, but in his mind, he wants to be a man. He needs respect, and you're treating him like he's still seven," Dale gently offered.

Carol stopped in her tracks. *Wow. How did I miss this? How many disagreements and heated arguments could have been avoided had I simply spoken to my son differently?*

After this realization, Carol started applying what she had learned about respecting her husband to her twelve-year-old son. She began to do simple and small things, like prefacing requests for doing chores with, "I know you have a plan for (mowing the yard, emptying the dishwasher, etc.)," being careful with corrective comments, asking questions instead of being directive, intentionally showing admiration, and asking permission to enter his world before offering advice ("Do you mind if I make a suggestion?"). Within three months, their relationship had done a 180.

Years later, when he was applying for colleges and jobs, Carol sat at her kitchen table with him as he filled out the forms, knowing that when he left, she was going to seriously miss him. What a miracle God had worked in their lives.

Hands wrapped around her coffee cup, Carol sighed contentedly as she thought about how her son had recently asked for advice about a personal issue he was struggling with. She had felt privileged to be in his world as a coach and advisor. She had her husband to credit for this, and her years-long study about how to respect him. While there was obviously a difference between her relationship with her husband and her relationship with her son, she knew that men were wired to respond to respect, and she was glad to have put in the time and effort to learn how to show that to her son.

> Bottom line: If you model the adult language of respect early, your kids will feel valued.

Both men and women deeply desire to be valued by others. Choose respect even as your children are just stepping into preadulthood, and you will improve your relationships now and in the future. Engaging in conversations and conflict respectfully can diffuse the potential for anger and frustration on the part of your kids.

We can often avoid making them defensive when we treat them

like we would treat a coworker when we have a difference of opinion. We still have the final say and authority, but they are more open to our position when they feel their thoughts have been heard. Often we can find a solution that works for both us and our child by treating them with respect.

What About You?

☐ What effort have you put into learning how to speak the language of respect? Do an online search on "What does the Bible say about respect?" You can also search "What is respectful behavior?" if you need further direction.

☐ Ask your children if they feel respected by you; then ask what you do that communicates respect to them, regardless of what they say to the first question. Make an effort to do more of that, if possible.

☐ What conflicts have you had with your teens or husband recently? Did you behave disrespectfully during them? If you did, go back and apologize, letting them know you are working on being more respectful.

☐ Sometimes just being aware of a Bible verse will show us things about ourselves we didn't know before. What was illuminated for you today with regard to the verses at the beginning of the dare? How can those verses impact your interactions?

☐ If you are struggling with the concept of respect in general, or if you haven't reviewed it in a while, take fifteen minutes to read through the helpful resources at http://www.NinaRoesner.com/for-wives/.

Pray with us:

O heavenly Father,

This idea of respecting my kids is not necessarily something I've thought about as a parent. I always thought of it in terms of them respecting me, because I am the older and wiser one. But You did make them separate beings, something I sometimes forget in the mother/child relationship.

The thought of respectfully allowing my children to have their own thoughts, desires, and choices scares me. I know as they grow they need to develop their own identities, and I need to respect that. Help me give appropriate privacy. Help me treat them with common courtesy. Help me apologize when I am wrong. Keep me from embarrassing them in front of their friends. When I make requests, help me be respectful of their commitments and activities. Help me model unselfish behavior, encouragement, and empathy, all important aspects of respect. Help me see how my behavior toward my children can either create safety or damage our relationship for the future. Help me build them up by giving them the respect they deserve as individuals You created. Help me teach them how precious all of Your children are. You are the one who knit them in my womb. You are their creator, not me. Help me cherish their uniqueness by respecting our differences.

In Jesus' name,
Amen.

 *Dare 7* STOP YOURSELF

The tongue has the power of life and death, and those who love it will eat its fruit.

—Proverbs 18:21

Therefore, as God's chosen people, holy and dearly loved, clothe your-selves with compassion, kindness, humility, gentleness and patience.

—Colossians 3:12

Jessica was angry, really angry! How dare her daughter embarrass her like that!

That morning after teaching the freshman Sunday school class, one of her students had asked to speak to Jessica in private. "Mrs. Cummins, I hate to come to you with this, but my parents said I should share this with you. I think you need to talk to Maggie if she hasn't already told you what is going on at school."

"What is it, Logan?"

"All I can say is that it involves a boy and I think you should know about it. It's not good."

After they parted ways, the anger came. "My daughter is shar-ing secrets with another kid? Logan's family knows what is going on, while I don't even have a clue. What kind of mother will they think I am?" she muttered.

Jessica was still fuming when she arrived home and approached Maggie. "Maggie, what is going on at school? Logan came to me this morning at church and told me something is going on between you and a boy. What is it that he thinks I need to know about?"

Maggie's face turned beet red. "Nothing I can talk about with you!" she shouted as she ran to her room, slamming the door.

"Come back here, young lady. You owe me an explanation!"

Suddenly Jessica stopped herself. *This is my child I'm standing here yelling at.*

Instead of following her daughter, she walked into her own bedroom. "Lord, forgive me for messing this up. I know I approached Maggie in anger. It just hurts so much to think that Logan's perfect family knows sordid details about my daughter." As tears started sliding down her cheeks, she reached for a tissue. The pause was long enough for her to hear His voice.

Jessica, this isn't about Logan's family. This is about Maggie and you. Given how you just responded to her, is Maggie wrong? Are you a safe person for her to talk with? And why are you imagining the worst about your daughter?

"Oh, Lord, I'm so sorry. Forgive me. Help me get this right! And please help Maggie, no matter what the situation is."

Later that evening, Jessica approached Maggie again. "Honey, I want you to know that I've been thinking about your comment earlier today about you not being able to share things with me. I think you're right. I haven't been a safe person for you to confide in, and it makes me sad. I promise you that I am going to work hard on not getting so emotional. I want you to feel like I am here for you and to know that I'm on your side." She paused. "I'm sorry you are hurting right now with whatever is going on at school with this boy. I'm praying for you. If you get to a place where you think you want to talk, I want you to know that I'm here. I promise to just listen and not pass judgement. Maggie, I do love you, and nothing you do will ever change that."

Three days later . . .

"Mom, can we talk? I don't know how to handle this situation at school . . ."

Bottom line: Calm emotions create respectful communication.

Reacting rather than thinking is how most of us respond in times of frustration or fear. However, it is precisely during these times when it is important to reconcile ourselves with God first. If you find yourself in a situation where you are angry or emotional, allow yourself time to get your emotions under control before engaging in the situation. Remember also that we live this life for the audience of One—God. Our goal should be to please Him, not to gain the approval of others. Focusing on other people's opinions instead of God's can get in the way of doing what is right.

What About You?

☐ Have you ever flung words at your teen and wished you could take them back afterward? How does keeping your emotions and temper in check during conflict model maturity for your children?

☐ Sometimes a Bible verse will illuminate a character trait about ourselves that we didn't realize before. What came to mind as you read today's verses?

☐ Jessica chose not to push the issue but to give her daughter permission to come to her later. Do you typically push the issues that your children choose not to share with you, or do you allow them their space? Which do you think is a healthier response, and why?

☐ Jessica reengaged with Maggie in humility, asking for forgiveness. Have you ever had similar interactions with your kids? Why or why not?

☐ How has the fear of others' evaluations caused you to react to your child? How has this struggle interfered with your parenting?

☐ What is one situation you have handled poorly in the past with your child that you should revisit and apologize for? Make a plan to reengage your child on this issue.

Practice how you are going to approach your teen by carefully choosing your words in front of a mirror. Do you raise your eyebrows or glare at your child? Are you hearing words that will ignite a fire? This will give you a good indication as to whether you are ready to face the issue.

When you are ready, ask God to calm your fears and give you the words that will create a nonthreatening environment. Your son or daughter, like your husband, needs to feel safe when interacting with you. If you sense your child becoming defensive during the discussion, stop. Create safety before proceeding. This is incredibly important, as your children will not share with you if they feel threatened.

A simple way to create safety is to point out the contrast between what your child might be thinking and what you are actually trying to do. You might say something like, "Are you worried that I'm trying to control your life? I'm not interested in doing that—it's not my intent to hover over you or get involved in all the details. I am only trying to walk alongside you as you navigate the difficult waters of the social interactions you are dealing with. I think I may have made you defensive. Can we try again?"

If you wait too long to create safety in the conversation, you often cannot undo the damage. Be aware of facial expressions, eye contact, and body language, and try to discern the emotions of the other person.

Be aware of your own emotions too. What makes you angry? What upsets you? If you find tension rising within yourself, tell your teen you need to take an emotional break, and let them know you will return when you can talk about the situation more calmly. Ask God to increase your awareness in this area so that you can avoid a "Jessica" reaction in the future.

Pray with us:

Heavenly Father,

How many times do I fail? I want to get this parenting piece right, but sometimes my emotions, my anger, and my tongue get in the way. So many times I jump to thinking the worst when my child's situation might not be nearly as bad as I imagine it. Help me come to You with my emotions before I unleash them on my child. Help me always remember that I am here to provide shelter and wisdom, not issue ultimatums and judgment. Help me give my kids the benefit of the doubt instead of assuming the worst. When my anger or tongue gets the best of me, help me humbly apologize. I want to bring life to my relationship with this child.

Lord, I also pray that You will give me the courage to ask my children if there have been any times in their lives when they haven't viewed me as safe. As my children are soon to be adults, I want to make sure we've worked through any "time bomb" memories that have put distance between us. I want an opportunity to reconcile those and work through them in a way that will bring healing. I'm asking You, Father, to bring potential parenting wrongs to my mind so that I can go back and make amends. May my apologies be just like it says in Proverbs, a honeycomb, sweet to the soul and healing to the bones.

In the name of Jesus, I pray,
Amen.

Dare 8 TAKE CARE OF THE TEMPLE

There remains, then, a Sabbath-rest for the people of God; for anyone who enters God's rest also rests from their works, just as God did from his. Let us, therefore, make every effort to enter that rest, so that no one will perish by following their example of disobedience.

—Hebrews 4:9–11

On the seventh day he rested from all his work.

—Genesis 2:2 MSG

The women sat around the restaurant table and commiserated. Christine resentfully said, "And so I just keep doing everything, because he never lifts a finger. That makes me a good wife, right? Waiting on my husband and kids, serving, working, giving them everything they want when they want it, so I can 'bring him good all the days of his life' and be a good mom. Yesterday I drove to school and back three times because people forgot things. I didn't get to work out because I was driving around for an extra two hours."

Josephine chimed in. "I quickly learned there weren't enough hours in the day to manage kids, home, school, laundry, dinner, yard work . . . I'm not sure when the 'creep' occurred. When we got married, we both worked full-time, and somehow we still managed to divide the chores and get everything done."

Angela said, "When we started having kids, it made sense for me to take on a more active role at home, because I was there more than he was. But when I tried to 'do it all' because some other wife told me that's how it worked, I quickly became busy, exhausted, irritable, and resentful. Did I mention I was exhausted?"

Libby, the oldest of the four women, leaned back in her chair. "Ladies," she began, "I have been where you are—and I'm not saying I have it all figured out—but do you mind if I share a few things I've learned that have helped with this?"

The other women eagerly nodded.

"Having four kids while working part-time made me realize I couldn't do everything for everyone. My husband and I sat down one day, and we divvied up the chores. As the kids got older, we started assigning specific ones to them. We have the chore list on the fridge, and no one gets to hang out with friends, borrow the car, or do any gaming until those chores are done daily. Every time one of our kids leaves the nest to go to college, Bill and I revisit the list with the other kids. We've passed some of the chores to the ones still at home, but we've also taken a few back.

"I also have a rule about forgotten things: once a semester, you get what I call 'a freebie,' but if you forget something and need me to bring it to you after that, it costs you $5. If you forget again, it's $10, and it keeps going up by $5 each time. I know that sounds harsh, but it teaches kids to be responsible. They learn to seriously weigh asking you to bring something they forgot, but more importantly, they become proactive about taking their things to school."

Bottom line: Take care of the temple, and everyone benefits.

As women with teenagers, we often find ourselves burning both ends of the candle, but it's important to note that a lack of sleep adds to women's health issues, both mentally and physically. It is not respectful to yourself, your family, or, most importantly, to God to not take good care of the temple of the Holy Spirit: you. As a woman, you will likely still feel more responsible for the home than others in your family do, but you aren't managing a show home. You are raising people to be independent and modeling self-compassion, which is crucial for healthy emotional growth. Know you not only don't have to "do it all," but you shouldn't. In the big picture, it's not good for you, nor is it good for your family.

Children who grow up in homes where they are waited on like royalty develop attitudes of entitlement and are not equipped for doing well as adults in life. They need the skills of cooking, cleaning, budgeting, time management, conflict resolution, basic home maintenance, and laundry, to name a few, so it is important to give them the opportunity to learn.

Another thing to note is that dad helping out around the house, regardless of how many hours he works away from the home, actually helps him connect with his kids. According to Dr. John Gottman, men who do housework have kids who do better socially and academically, and they have better relationships with their wives.[1]

It is important for both parents to model doing chores and work alongside their kids. Typically, daughters repeat what they see their moms doing and sons repeat what they see dad doing. Remember that what you model—including balance and self-care—is what your children are most likely to do, regardless of the lectures you give.

What About You?

☐ If this is an area you could use some help with, what lie are you believing that keeps you from respecting and giving compassion to yourself? In prayer, ask God to reveal the earliest moment in your life when you came to believe that lie and to show you what is really true instead of what you perceived. Ask Him what He wants you to know— and listen. He may bring to mind a verse that helps you understand. Feel free to ask Him for confirmation, and trust that He will do this.

☐ What skills does the average adult need to do well in life? Are your tweens and teens developing these skills, or are you doing too much for them? Where do you see yourself getting in the way of your children's growth? Why do you think you are doing that?

☐ Meet with your husband, and talk through the many chores that need to happen to keep your home clean and maintained. If he's open, ask him if he would choose some to model for the kids. Set up a schedule for taking care of projects around the house together.

☐ Together with your children, establish reasonable rules (i.e., what has to happen before certain privileges are given—TV, gaming, friends, etc.). Have the kids participate in setting the rules and the chore system (e.g., having one of them run a team meeting to discuss this).

Let the kids know the chore topic will be revisited approximately two to three times a year when they'll be able to change responsibilities, or have them suggest a rotation based on what is on the list.

Put everyone's new assignments and what the rules are in a clear format on the refrigerator, and start managing the system.

☐ If you have a hobby or activity that recharges your batteries, make sure you regularly schedule time to participate in it.

☐ If you grow in the areas discussed above, what will change in your life as a result?

Pray with us:

My precious Savior,

Rescue me from myself. I'll admit that sometimes I do things myself rather than wrestle over who is doing what chore and checking to see if they got it done well. I also find myself running at my children's beck and call, bailing them out because I want them to succeed. Sometimes it is just easier. But, Lord, Your Word says that even You rested. You even commanded the Israelites to rest so that they could be refreshed. Thank You for permission to rest.

Lord, help me engage my husband's support in determining how we can better train our children. I want to create a sense of unity that is always looking out for the needs of our family, which includes our home and, yes, even me. Lord, I know that I won't always be there to pick up their dirty socks or take what they need to them at work or school. I don't want to leave that legacy to their future spouses. Help us know what systems we need to put in place and in what ways we can help develop our children's sense of ownership and maturity through the chores we give them. Give us a well-thought-out plan that will make our home a place of peace and rest.

I recognize that following up will most likely become my new responsibility. Help me be diligent in this effort so that my children can learn to be responsible for themselves but also for their own families when they are grown. Give me patience, Lord, when they don't do things to my standard. Help me persevere in running the race just like Paul suggested in 1 Corinthians.

Jesus, I pray all these things in Your name,
Amen.

Dare 9 COUNTER THE CULTURE

"On the day when I act," says the LORD Almighty, "they will be my treasured possession. I will spare them, just as a father has compassion and spares his son who serves him."

—MALACHI 3:17

"Do not conform to the pattern of this world, but be transformed by the renewing of your mind. Then you will be able to test and approve what God's will is—his good, pleasing and perfect will."

—ROMANS 12:2

Marilyn and her daughter, Rachel, were shopping when Rachel gawked, "Did you just see that?"

Marilyn looked at Rachel's smiling face. "See what?"

"That boy. He totally thinks I'm pretty! He looked at me and smiled!"

"How does that make you feel?" inquired Marilyn.

"Special. Important. Beautiful."

Marilyn quietly sighed and prayed for wisdom. *How do I interact with this, Lord?*

She was familiar with this kind of response to attention. Leading a women's Bible study at her church, she frequently spoke to grown women, who, just like her daughter, ached inside for the attention of a man. What was the best way to address the beginnings of this misplaced desire in her own daughter?

Marilyn knew she needed wisdom. Her friend Paula had four

teenage girls who were older than Rachel and was often a great source of advice. After spending some time with Paula, Marilyn felt empowered to talk with her daughter.

"Rachel," Marilyn ventured one evening a few days later as they went for a walk. "Remember the other day when we were shopping and that boy looked at you and smiled?"

"Yeah. He was dreamy," Rachel sighed, spinning around.

"I know you enjoyed getting his attention. Most women enjoy the attention of a man. In fact, some women get their identity from the attention of others. They even buy cool or expensive clothes, or sometimes clothes that reveal a little too much, to get others' attention."

"I've seen that too. Did you see Sophie's top the other day at church? You could see cleavage."

"Yes, honey, I did. What did you think about that?"

"I couldn't believe her mom let her go out of the house with that on. All the guys kept staring at her chest."

"How did that make you feel?"

"Uncomfortable, I guess. But she certainly got a lot of attention."

"Is that the way you would want to get attention?"

"Hmm . . . I guess not."

"You know, Rachel, God created in you a desire to be seen and accepted by others, but I'm hoping you will find your identity in God, taking pleasure in who you are on the inside rather than how a guy sees your outward beauty. I know that the world sees things differently, but I hope that over the next several years we'll have more dialogue about how to think about and respond to a guy's attention."

> Bottom line: Engage in the culture war, and you can positively influence your child's sense of identity.

It's important to be vigilant about speaking the truth of how God sees our kids to offset the messages coming from outside.

Starting the conversation about identity as soon as our children start noticing the other sex will allow for more influence as they head into the dating years. If we start even younger by affirming our kids and ourselves for positive character traits—and not spending too much time focusing on things we don't like about our appearance, dwelling on our failures, or shaming ourselves when we make mistakes—we'll be emphasizing the right things as a counter against the loud voice of the culture. If we approach it like an argument, though, our children will discount what we offer up. Instead, we must gently, lovingly, and truthfully speak light into our children's lives. We cannot give up, no matter how frequently we battle misdirection.

It helps to be clear with kids from a very early age that this world wants to separate them from God, but even if we haven't done that yet, we can start now. Our kids need to learn to be smart about what they choose to listen to, watch on TV, read, play on the computer, access on their smartphone, and even about the people they choose to have as close friends. We can't keep our kids in a bubble—completely isolating them from temptation usually backfires—but kids need to learn to how to deal with culture in the safest environment they have—home—and we need to do our best to insure that the amount of biblical truth they absorb exceeds the amount of secular influence they face.

What About You?

- [ ] In what do you base your identity? Do you live life for the audience of One, or do you seek approval from culture, your friends, etc.?
- [ ] What are you teaching your kids about who they are and how to base their identities in what God thinks instead of the world's definition?

☐ What are you modeling for your kids in terms of the influences you allow in your home? Do you have greater exposure to Christian and faith-based influences or to secular TV, media, Internet, music, magazines, etc. What do you sense God leading you to do in this area?

☐ What type of friends are you coaching your kids to hold close to their hearts? While we need to be an influence on the world, those we are closest to need to be people with similar core values. How are you and your kids doing in this area?

☐ How often do you discuss faith-based issues with your children and talk about how to build your relationship with God? Are you modeling what you want your children to do in this area, or are you too focused on gaining approval from others?

☐ Take inventory of how you are doing regarding regularly choosing biblical truth first. Perhaps even check in with your kids after doing so, and begin an ongoing dialogue about these things. Level with your kids, if necessary, if you have regrets about what you've allowed them to be exposed to and why it matters. Have an open discussion about what you can all do as a family to encourage more holy attitudes and behaviors in this area. Choose from this day forward to interact with your kids about these things without being judgmental.

Pray with us:

Dear Father,

This world exposes children to too much too quickly. I never cease to be amazed at how I seem to get blindsided by yet another thing I need to discuss with my children. This journey is hard, Lord. Finding balance between what my kids want to do and what they should be allowed to do is difficult enough, but the technology, the media, and the boy/girl thing can quickly point them down the wrong path. I want You to have their hearts. I want them to have their identity in You. Why do I so easily forget that at times?

Sometimes I don't even want to recognize my own faults and failures when it comes to modeling a healthy identity in You. Forgive me, Lord. Help me learn ways to grow closer to You so that my kids will see my relationship with You. Help me initiate dialogue that always points back to You. Help me establish healthy boundaries between overexposure to the world and underexposure to the things that could hit them hard in the future if they haven't encountered them in the safety of our home. And most of all, Lord, give us grace in our parenting.

In the precious name of Jesus,
Amen.

REFRAIN FROM CASTING BLAME

But you, LORD, are a compassionate and gracious God, slow to anger, abounding in love and faithfulness.

—PSALM 86:15

Sitting in her comfy chair, Gail had cloistered herself in her bedroom to talk on the phone with a friend who had recently moved away. "Things are good," she said as she caught Jane up on all the news. Her oldest was working full-time, Elizabeth was away at college, and Daniel was in the TV room playing video games with his friend Alex. As the conversation continued, someone kept beeping in on the other line, but Gail ignored it the first two times, savoring this time with her friend. By the third time, though, she figured she'd better answer it.

"Gail, where's Daniel?" Her husband sounded scared on the other end of the phone.

"In his room with Alex," she responded. "Sorry I didn't pick up the first time you called. I have Jane on the other line."

"Gail, I just got a text from Alex's dad. He says he overheard Alex and Daniel saying they were going to get high today. It's National Weed Day."

"Is he sure? Daniel was only gone for about fifteen minutes when he went to pick up Alex. He came right back home. I don't think they had time to do something like that. Has Alex's dad ever seen Daniel smoking pot?"

"I'm not sure what is going on. It doesn't surprise any of us that

Alex goes out and smokes weed, but I don't think Daniel would. Still, kids do stupid stuff. I'll call Steve while you check on Daniel and Alex. I'll call you back."

As Gail said a quick good-bye to Jane, her heart started racing. "Lord, You know the truth. Whatever is going on, help me discover truth! This doesn't sound like our son. Also, help me remain calm." With that, Gail started off on her mission to get to the truth. She checked every crevice of the car and found no evidence, nor was there a hint of odor. *Steve has to be mistaken. The boys were probably just joking around like crazy teenagers*, she thought.

Next she knocked on the unlocked door to the TV room, quickly opening it before the boys would have time to put anything away. Sure enough, they were both entranced in their game and didn't seem to have anything to hide. *Hmm . . . nothing suspicious here.* After offering the boys a snack, she exited when she heard the phone ring.

"What did you find?" Glenn asked.

"Not a thing. I checked the car, the TV room, and I even put my hand on Daniel's shoulder trying to get a good whiff. I smelled and saw absolutely nothing."

"Steve said about a year ago, when Daniel was dropping off Alex at his house, Daniel rolled down the window to say hi, and Steve thought he smelled pot. He didn't actually see anything, but he thought Daniel had been smoking."

"Glenn, you know Steve as well as I do. His boys have been into some pretty deep stuff, and he tends to think the worst about them. Some of it is justified, and I do feel somewhat uncomfortable about Daniel hanging out with Alex. That's why Daniel and I have an agreement about the amount of time he can spend with Alex and I usually insist that they hang out here, but I really think Daniel has a point. How can he win Alex over if we keep them separated? Those two have been friends since third grade. Daniel cares about the choices Alex is making. At some point, we have to let go and trust God."

"Yeah, okay. I have to trust your judgment on this since I'm out of town. Just keep your eyes open, though, will you? Keep me posted if you suspect anything."

> Bottom line: Get the facts before taking action, and you'll avoid falsely accusing your kids.

If we strive to parent like our heavenly Father does, we must be compassionate and gracious, long-suffering and abundant in mercy and truth. As our teens get older and are on their own more and more, we may hear things from others that may or may not be true. Typically, when something of magnitude surfaces, we tend to allow fear to overcome us or jump to conclusions. Rather than operate out of fear, however, search for truth, and remember we can trust that God knows what is going on—even if He allows something difficult to happen in our kids' lives. He loves them more than we could ever even dream of, and He means everything for their good.

When you hear something that concerns you, think about how your child typically handles these types of situations. Give your teen the benefit of the doubt—this is respectful and will prevent painful accusations. You may, in fact, find that your teen is guilty. Regardless, deal with your child from a place of compassion and mercy, hoping that he or she sees God's grace and firm love, which will only help in the long run.

What About You?

☐ What boundaries have you set up with your kids about spending time with friends who might get them involved in unsavory things? Did you lay down the law, or did you reach a consensus? How has your tween or teen responded to these boundaries?

☐ Ask your teens what they think you think of them. Do they feel you hold them in high esteem, think they are responsible, give them the benefit of the doubt, trust them, etc.? Ask what it is you do that communicates these things.

☐ Did your parents accuse you when you were a teen or did they give you the benefit of the doubt and discuss issues calmly with you? Has this influenced your parenting? How?

☐ Has anyone come to you about the behavior of one of your kids? Did you believe what the person said about your child? Did you make assumptions about his or her guilt or innocence? Did you become defensive? Why or why not?

☐ How defensive do accusations like this make you? Why do you think that is?

Pray with us:

Heavenly Father,

Psalms says that You are gracious and compassionate, slow to anger and rich in love. I love my children and want to be slow to reach that point of anger. There are so many times I automatically jump to the wrong conclusion when someone says something negative about my child. I either judge the person or my kid instead of just seeking Your truth. It is easy to think the worst. Lord, I know Your Word tells me to be careful about the measure I use to judge. Help me lean toward grace with everyone.

There are so many things that can put me in fear mode with the kids. Drugs, alcohol, pornography, and sex are only a few of the pitfalls that seem to entice this generation. Lord, my prayer is that You will spare my family from having to deal with the potential consequences of such behavior, but I also realize it is naive to think that it can't happen to me.

If, or maybe I should say when, these potential dangers rear their ugly head, help me build a bridge between myself and my child rather than put up a wall of anger. Give me strength and help, and let me not give way to fear. I know that You are always with me, because You are my God. Hold me with Your hand of righteousness. Give me strength to claim Your promise for my family. I know that You have plans for us to prosper; these plans are not to harm us but to give us a hope and a future. Help me always call upon You whenever I start to give way to fear, knowing You will always be there in my time of need.

In the name of Jesus,
Amen.

Dare 11 **SPEAK THE TRUTH**

The Spirit you received does not make you slaves, so that you live in fear again; rather, the Spirit you received brought about your adoption to sonship. And by him we cry, "Abba, Father." The Spirit himself testifies with our spirit that we are God's children.

—ROMANS 8:15–16

B reathing deeply, Tai held the phone away from her face and turned the volume down a little. The mom on the other end of the line continued her rant, venting about Tai's son, Brenden, and his interaction with the woman's daughter, who was Brenden's girl-friend. Details about how wonderful the girl was, how important it was that she make the most of this year because "high school is everything!" went on and on . . .

"Mika can't get her homework done! She has AP classes and is in the show choir! She works part-time! Your son keeps her on the phone all hours of the night, and he's not hearing her hints when she tells him she needs to get off and do homework. This is high school—she's going to have problems if she can't do a good job on all the things she's involved with right now!"

Tai sensed a pause for the first time in nearly ten minutes and quickly entered the conversation, having already prayed extensively about what God would have her do. *Speak the truth in love*, she'd heard.

"Kayla, it sounds like you are really frustrated—" she began.

The woman interrupted. "Of course I'm frustrated! Haven't you been listening? I'm trying to explain to you that you need to tell your son to stop calling my daughter so much and to not be on the phone so long!"

"Kayla, I hear that you are frustrated with this, and if I understand you correctly, you are concerned that Mika's grades, her role in show choir, and her job are going to suffer because of the time she spends on the phone with Brenden. Is that right?" Tai offered up.

"Well, it sounds like you finally are getting it!" Kayla's voice calmed a bit.

Tai asked God to turn the small flame of irritation into compassion for this other mom. She clearly had her identity wrapped up in her daughter's experience of high school. "I'm glad you feel like I hear you," she began again. "If it's okay with you, I'd like to offer up something that may not fit exactly with what you are suggesting, but if you will hear me out, you might find it helpful."

"Okay, go ahead," came the reply.

"When my kids were around ten to twelve years old, I slowly stopped inserting myself into their interactions with other kids and managing their relationships in a hands-on way. Instead, I started taking on the role of coach or advisor, because I wanted my kids to be able to successfully live independently as adults. I encourage you to talk with your daughter, gently nudging her to speak with my son about what he's doing that's bothering her. I think they'd both feel more respected if I didn't try to manage his behavior, and I also think they'd both get some great experience in dealing with conflict," Tai explained.

"Are you kidding me? Why on earth would you suggest that? Your son needs a knot jerked in his tail, and you need to do it! I can't believe you let your kids deal with things on their own! Nobody does that! You should just tell him he isn't allowed to be on the phone more than an hour," came the heated reply.

"Kayla, I understand that this isn't a super common way of dealing with things, and I'm sorry the way I am handling it is upsetting to you. I love your daughter and respect her a lot. I'd like to see others, especially boys, respect her too. I'd like to see her respect herself by being more confident in the way she interacts with my son. Mika's going to college next year, right? So is Brenden. Mika needs to have a strong 'no' if she's going to be away at school. Otherwise she's going to find herself in situations where she gets taken advantage of. Brenden needs to learn to hear 'no' or 'stop' and respect it. Neither you nor I are going to be on campus with them to manage their relationships next year, and this is a great opportunity for both of them to have some adult interaction with each other now. I'm sorry to tell you no, but I'm not going to insert myself into their issue. If Brenden wants advice on how to handle this, I'm happy to talk with him, but I'm not going to tell him he has a problem with his girlfriend, nor am I going to make rules to fix things in your home for you," Tai said calmly.

"So you aren't going to do anything?" Kayla asked, sounding shocked.

"No, I'm not. I appreciate how you feel about your daughter's situation, and I think you've done a great job raising her. She's bright and capable, and I think she will handle this situation with Brenden just fine," Tai replied.

"I don't know if she will," Kayla said. "How do you trust them that much?"

"I have to. God loves them more than I do, and I have to let them figure out how to do life. I want my kids to feel like I helped them instead of did things for them."

"Well, I don't agree with your approach, but I can't make you do anything. So I guess I'm done here." Kayla hung up.

Tai prayed and thanked God for the freedom He'd shown her by releasing her from her obsessions with perfection and pleasing people. She prayed Kayla and her kids would find this freedom as well. Her heart had beaten a little faster during their conversation and Kayla's words had stung a bit, but nothing like they would have years ago. Well, maybe those words would never have even been said years ago, because Tai wouldn't have been brave enough to speak up in the first place. She would have been too concerned about what Kayla thought about her and her son!

Tai sat back and smiled. She'd grown. She could see it. This felt like an achievement!

> Bottom line: Stand firm in how you parent, and you will show respect for yourself and your kids.

Choosing freedom from the opinions of others helps us speak the truth in love and stay out of God's way as He works to grow those around us. We live in a culture designed to enable children in immaturity (think "helicopter parenting") instead of equipping them for adulthood. We steal opportunities for growth from our kids and from God when we try to control their behavior, shooting for perfection so we will be well thought of, which is the sin of pride. Fear of rejection or judgment causes us to interfere with God's plans for us to allow our kids to bear their own loads and mature. Yes, we should walk with them and share their burdens, but completely carrying their burdens for them is not what He intends. This stunts their growth. And we sin when we do not give them the opportunity to develop the life skills they need. Our goal is to respectfully launch our children, allowing them to learn from their interactions with others without our interference.

What About You?

☐ In the story, Tai did a good job of listening to the other parent but gently and respectfully communicating her boundaries. How do you feel about what she did? Would it have been harder for you to voice your thoughts or to earnestly and kindly listen? Would you ultimately have intervened in the children's situation in response to what Kayla said? When have you found it difficult to choose valuing God's opinion over others' demands?

☐ For Tai, speaking the truth in love and not giving in to Kayla's desires for her to do something to fix the problem felt like a victory. What would you consider a victory or achievement in your life? This is something you have worked hard to accomplish over time and have (whether known to you at the time or not) received God's help in accomplishing. Perhaps you were able to heal a relationship, learned how to speak the truth in love (like the story in this dare), or completed a household project. If you have difficulty coming up with an example, ask your husband, sister, or good friend if they have witnessed you diligently pursuing a goal. You could also ask God for direction. Write down the details of that event.

☐ Record all the aspects of the situation. Prayerfully make notes about how you thought about the challenges you faced, how you overcame them, what your thought patterns were like, etc. Did you celebrate the event?

☐ What do you sense God wants you to know about yourself based on this victory? What do you sense God wants you to know about Him based on this achievement?

☐ Speaking of achievement, go back to Dare 1. How are you positively different now compared to then, even if it is just in awareness?

☐ If you are doing this with a small group, what growth have you already seen in others?

☐ Write "Whatever we pay attention to grows" on a 3 x 5

card, and put it where you can see it daily to remind you to look for what God would say is true, noble, right, pure, lovely, admirable, praiseworthy, and excellent in yourself and others. Then give voice to these things, thanking God for helping you see life through the lens of the Holy Spirit.

Pray with us:

Dear precious Lord,

There are so many times when I step into my children's business when I should be letting them work through it on their own. Help me be aware when I should be standing on the sidelines and coaching rather than getting in the middle of their day-to-day lives. Help me also live by my convictions rather than allow other moms to push me into solving their problems with their child because of interactions with my kid. I want to respect the fact that my children are growing up. I want them to learn to navigate the world of human interaction on their own with different personalities rather than to depend on me to be the middleman in their interactions with others.

Oh, Lord, this idea of growth in myself as a parent is something I haven't thought too much about. Sometimes I feel like my identity is so wrapped up in what my kids accomplish that I forget to work on me. I also don't take time to acknowledge when I do something brave. I want to accomplish the goals I've set for myself. Help me become more aware of these and celebrate each small step. Complete this work in me so that others will see You through our family.

In Jesus' name,
Amen.

Dare 12 PARENT WITH PERSPECTIVE

"Judge not, that you be not judged. For with what judgment you judge, you will be judged; and with the measure you use, it will be measured back to you."

—MATTHEW 7:1–2 NKJV

"And the two will become one flesh. So they are no longer two, but one flesh. Therefore what God has joined together, let no one separate."

—MARK 10:8–9

Paula stood next to the toaster in her kitchen. It was 5:00 a.m. She was so angry she could scream.

She also knew she was wrong and needed to apologize. She knew her retort had spewed venom, but all she could focus on was how her husband's words had stung. She had to admit, though, that he was right; she had placed their daughter's needs above his. But did he need to respond so curtly?

She was mad at herself for blowing it, but she was also angry and hurt. Yes, she had spent a good amount of time with Ava and the dance team and the other kids might be jealous, but she also felt like her husband didn't get it. She was frustrated with him for not understanding. She wanted to enjoy her daughter without being made to feel guilty.

Even so, while she didn't feel it, she knew the next right thing God would have her do. It was time for humble pie.

As she wrote the note, apologizing, her heart was not yet in alignment with the words, but she allowed the Holy Spirit to guide her pen.

> I'm sorry, Martin, for the distance I've created between the two of us. I know you want what is best for Ava as well as the rest of the family. I'll admit that I've been focused on Ava's success with the dance team. I see such potential for her, and it warms my heart to see all the awards she receives as a result of her obvious giftedness. She positively glows when she is on stage, so when she is chosen for solos it's hard to say no. I know that most of my weekends are tied up with travel with the team, but I don't want to miss a moment of her success. We agreed I would travel with her. I guess I didn't realize how much that would entail and how it would impact the rest of the family.
>
> You are right in that I've not been tuned into our marriage as much as I should be. I guess I've just been thinking of this time with Ava as a season of life that will soon be gone. I know you and I will always be here after she graduates in a few years.
>
> Please forgive me for not looking at the big picture of our family and our marriage. Can we talk tonight around 8:00 when I get home? I'd like to talk through what you are feeling and what happened this morning. We also need to talk about Ava's commitment to the team. I do love you.

After she put the note on the dashboard of Martin's car, she went to her room to pray.

"Teach me, Father. I feel like I am the one who always has to apologize first. I hate it when he hurls words at me that sting. Can't we just have a conversation about what is bothering him rather than making me feel like a verbal punching bag? His anger gets so out of control. I want to feel cherished by him. I want us to discuss simple family decisions rather than receive ultimatums."

And then Genesis 2 came to mind. *He needs your help . . . he is not complete without you,*[1] the familiar voice spoke to her heart.

Then, *"And why do you look at the speck in your brother's eye, but do not consider the plank in your own eye? Or how can you say to your brother, 'Let me remove the speck from your eye'; and look, a plank is in your own eye? Hypocrite! First remove the plank from your own eye, and then you will see clearly to remove the speck from your brother's eye."*[2]

"Oh, Lord, you are so right. I'm feeling like Martin is being selfish for wanting me home all the time, but maybe I'm being selfish for wanting to be with Ava so much. I guess I have put her above him, above the rest of the kids, above You. Lord, how can I show him how much his words hurt? It makes me want to be away from him. Life is better at the dance studio. I get to enjoy the experience rather than feel like I am always needed or have something to do or am going to disappoint him yet again."

As Paula let the words she had just spoken sink into her heart, she sensed God's presence.

Parenting takes two perspectives. The kids need to see you parenting together—not separately.

"Thank You for showing me this, Lord. Help Martin and me learn not only to respectfully keep our tongues in check, but help us learn to be on the same page as we parent, willing to listen to the other's opinion."

The salt-seasoned dish of grace calmed her heart, and her swollen and bruised ego vanished. She found herself looking forward to her discussion with Martin later that night. They were on this journey of parenting together, and they needed to learn how to best do it as a team. Paula chose to extend the same grace to herself and her husband and to ask God to fill her with His grace for everyone in her family more consistently.

Bottom line: Choose humility, and you are more likely to parent in agreement.

Parenting during the tween and teen years can sometimes wreak havoc on marriage communication. Scripture tells us in Genesis that the "two shall become one"[3] and we need to remember that also applies in the context of parenting. Even if we are separated or divorced, we will still, at some point, find ourselves in situations where we are co-parenting and disagree with the other party. We can potentially avoid conflict with our husbands or co-parents if we handle these situations of relationship collision better.

It is easy as parents to get so focused on our own desires or pride in what we want for ourselves or a particular child that we can easily lose a bigger family perspective. But God can help us keep our focus on our own behavior during times of conflict if we approach our spouse or co-parent with humility and learn to rely on God for introspection.

It is important that we model a sense of family for our children. Tweens and teens need to see that their mom and dad have conflict but can resolve it well. They also need to see that family is the highest priority, not just mom and child.

A day will come when our kids leave the nest. It is important that they have a sense of family to return home to.

What About You?

☐ It is important that we not only initiate conversation often on how we are going to co-parent but also be mindful of our husband's hot buttons. What are the things you know are precious to him? What parenting philosophy does he embrace that greatly differs with your desires? Do you side with your child instead of with him? When your child has a request, does your husband want you to consult him?

☐ Ask God and yourself whether you often choose your

child's desires instead of your husband's. Do you have a particular child whom you seem to pour into more than the others? Ask your husband for his perspective.

☐ What parameters have you set up in your life that enable you to spend time with God reading His Word, thanking Him for what He has given you, asking Him for guidance, praying for others, and listening to Him for direction? What can you do to create an environment or structure in your life that facilitates time with Him on a daily basis?

☐ When has God helped you see a situation differently? Did you thank Him? Take a few moments now to give Him appreciation for guiding your steps and transforming your mind.

☐ Where in your family do you see potential areas of jealousy? How could you use empathy, compassion, and apology to restore things in a healthier way?

☐ What do you sense God wanting you to do with this? How did today's verse impact what you sense from Him? What action are you going to take based on what He has revealed to you?

Pray with us:

Almighty God,

I want to be like the tree planted by streams of water that yields its fruit in season and whose leaf does not wither. May the watering of relationships in my home cause them to prosper. Help me delight in You, Lord, and help me meditate on Your Word day and night. It is so easy to look side to side, sizing up how I am doing based on how I feel others are doing. Surround me with women who will teach me what it is like to have mercy on others so that I can model that in my home and in other relationships.

Help me stand strong and choose grace and forgiveness in all circumstances. In a home of sinful people, there is so much opportunity to feel as if I am the person who is always right. Humble me, and open my eyes to see other perspectives. When I am in error, give me the strength and humility to apologize, and when I have been wronged, help me forgive those who sin against me just like You forgive me, as You command us to do in Scripture. When I am hurt at other's reactions, help me always offer an apology and forgiveness. Help me model this for my children so they will see Christ in me.

In Jesus' name,
Amen.

Dare 13   LEAP OUTSIDE YOUR COMFORT ZONE

Be strong and courageous. Do not be afraid or terrified because of them, for the LORD your God goes with you; he will never leave you nor forsake you.

—DEUTERONOMY 31:6

"I have told you these things, so that in me you may have peace. In this world you will have trouble. But take heart! I have overcome the world."

—JOHN 16:33

"Are you all right, honey?" Sheila gasped as she put her arms around her daughter.

Rebecca only looked at her with a blank stare as she continued to wrap herself in a ball and sob. Sheila felt helpless as she watched her daughter rocking back and forth as though she were in a trance.

"Rebecca, honey, can you tell me what's going on?"

Back and forth Rebecca rocked, Sheila rubbing her back and trying to get through to her.

"Lord," Sheila whispered. "Help me know what to do! I've never seen her this way. Calm her and give her peace. Please, Lord!"

For what seemed like an eternity, the scene continued. It was after midnight on a Saturday night as Sheila sat with her daughter, trying to figure out what could have possibly happened. What could have made Rebecca so distraught?

She had gone out with Andy and some other friends just like she usually did on Saturday evenings. When Rebecca came home, she'd said good night and gone up to her room. But then she had heard what sounded like crying coming from Rebecca's room, and Sheila had entered to find her daughter in the position she was in now.

Suddenly, Rebecca sprang to life. "Mom, you've got to let me go to Andy's house. I know it is after midnight, but I have to go!"

"Rebecca, it is too late for you to go over there now. What is going on that can't wait until the morning?"

Then the story spilled out. Andy had broken up with her that evening. They had gotten into what she considered a small disagreement, and within minutes he had told her he didn't like her anymore and never wanted to see her again. He had also said some other pretty nasty things.

"But, Mom, I have to see him tonight! You just don't understand! I have to see him tonight!" Rebecca yelled through her tears.

Sheila attempted to reason with her daughter, but she didn't seem to be getting through to her. Then Rebecca jumped up and headed toward the door, announcing that she would just walk there if she had to. Sheila grabbed her coat, shoes, and keys.

"Lord, this is crazy!" she gasped. "I can't believe this is happening! Help us."

After driving Rebecca to Andy's house where he met her outside, Sheila watched as they talked and saw that Rebecca had become visibly calmer.

"So tell me where things are between you and Andy," she ventured when Rebecca got back in the car.

"Mom, Andy said we'd talk about it tomorrow, and then he gave me a hug. I think it will work out."

As Sheila shared the story with their church's counseling pastor the next day, she asked what he thought she might be dealing with.

"You know, Sheila, some kids have stronger feelings than

normal. They find their identity in other people rather than who God created them to be. Thankfully, they eventually grow up, and their emotions become more stabilized. Our job is to be there for them as best we can. Last night must have been difficult, but you are a good mom. You were there for your daughter."

Bottom line: Courageous empathy creates stronger connection.

Fear of loneliness plagues our young people today. One of their greatest needs is to feel like they belong. In a world where they are so connected with texting and instant messaging, sometimes close relationships don't have time to blossom. When they do and then get disrupted, our teens may not be emotionally prepared to handle it. To suddenly be told "you are not what I'm looking for" can be devastating.

Handling emotional situations can be difficult for any parent. Research shows that on average, moms are typically more emotionally in tune with their children, as Sheila displayed in her response to Rebecca. Dads, on the other hand, don't usually have the same emotional tendency toward empathy and comfort. On average, men's brains are wired to fix the problem. Sometimes when they do that, though the problem may go away, they end up damaging the relationship. That's why it might be wise for women to help their husband interact with the teen, while also considering his input.[1] As a mom, if we have received feedback that we need to show more empathy, obviously we need to grow in this area, too, keeping in mind that gender research is not absolute. We will all face times where we don't know what to do. Our teen or tween can react in emotional ways that seem extreme in our adult world. But we must remember that our job is to let our children know we are there to walk beside them. We may not always support what's happening in a particular situation, but our teens need to know we support *them*.

What About You?

☐ Have you ever experienced a situation where your teen seemed to respond in an over-the-top emotional manner? If so, what was your response?

☐ How did your response help or hinder the relationship? What have you learned from that interaction?

☐ After reading Sheila's story, do you think she handled things wisely? Why or why not? If not, what could she have done differently?

☐ Sheila's situation took time and energy. Do you think you would have the tenacity to sit with your child if they needed you? If not, what would it take for you to be there for your teen no matter what?

☐ Think of the last emotional situation your teen was involved in that you wish you would have handled better. In prayer, ask God to help you discern where you got off track and why, and what you could have done and when (like Sheila listening without taking it personally when Rebecca started yelling). Ask Him for help in doing better next time. Talk through this situation with your teen, apologizing and letting your teen know how you wish you would have handled things.

Pray with us:

Gracious Father,

There are so many times in parenting that I don't know what to do. When my children are emotionally distraught, I want to help get them to the other side of the emotion. Give me wisdom about when to intervene and when to let them work through things on their own. Your Word says not to be anxious about anything. Help me teach my children that when they are overwhelmed with emotion, they can turn to You. Philippians says that when we are anxious, we are to present our requests to You by prayer and petition with thanksgiving, and You will give us peace that transcends all understanding. Lord, I need to remember that for myself as well.

Also, Lord, sometimes I don't display the patience that my children need from me. I get busy and sometimes just don't want to deal with their crisis. Give me a heart of compassion during these situations so that I can best reflect You to my children.

In the precious name of Jesus,
Amen.

ENCOURAGE RATHER THAN NAG

"Teacher, which is the greatest commandment in the Law?"

*Jesus replied: "Love the L*ORD *your God with all your heart and with all your soul and with all your mind.' This is the first and greatest commandment. And the second is like it: 'Love your neighbor as yourself.'"*

—MATTHEW 22:36–39

Julie needed to apologize to her seventeen-year-old for losing her cool over his lack of motivation to finish his college applications. She had been encouraging him to work on them for months, and now the deadline had arrived and they were due the next day.

She knew she had started the conversation disrespectfully by "mothering him" (otherwise known as nagging). She hadn't really tried to understand what he was dealing with and what might be affecting the situation. At one point, he honestly told her, "Mom, the more you talk, the more you try to get me to do this, the less I want to."

Ouch, but true. In her efforts, she had failed to encourage and had become the opposite: discouraging. But there was still a quandary. He had to apply—today or tomorrow—or he would miss the deadline. And she had to help him see that clearly without making him not want to do it—again.

So she attempted apologizing three times, making things a bit worse each time rather than better. Finally, she went into her son's room and sat on the edge of his bed. "Look, I'm not doing this well.

And you're right, I've been a nag. And I'm sorry. I don't want to do that, but I also want you to get your college applications in. What's going on here? Why is it so hard for you to get it done?" she asked.

Then she listened. And she found out how scared he was. Filling out the applications meant high school was over, that everything was going to change. He didn't want it to. His friends, his school, his job—he wished it would all stay the same. Filling out the paperwork meant everything was going to be different next year.

This time, instead of arguing and telling him why he was wrong, or telling him to "get over it and grow up," Julie empathized. "Oh, honey. I get that. It does seem like it's all going to change, doesn't it? What do you love most right now?"

Again she listened to him, agreed with him, and let him be where he was.

"I'm sorry I haven't listened better to you," she offered.

"It's okay," he said. "I haven't really known what the deal was until today."

"So if I understand what you're saying, you're feeling . . ." And then Julie spent several minutes talking about what he'd said and how he was feeling. He corrected her a few times on minor points, but overall, she understood what he was trying to communicate.

"Yeah, that's about it," he acknowledged.

"I remember being your age and dealing with similar things," she began as she shared her story of moving across the United States to go to school, feeling terrified and alone.

He seemed to be listening, and his face softened. "That had to have been hard."

"Oh, it was, but I had my old friends praying for me. And we stayed in touch; a lot of them came to my wedding."

"That's cool."

"How can I pray for you?" she asked.

"I don't know, maybe that I'll get the courage to do it anyway. I know high school isn't going to go on forever, but I wish it would."

"What are you going to do?" she asked.

"I don't know," he said.

"Would it help if I sat with you while you filled out the forms?"

"Yeah, okay," he said.

And so that's what they did. Just as her husband often wanted her to be in his company while he completed a task, her son needed something similar. Julie was grateful that she had realized her son just needed to be listened to and encouraged, and she was glad she could be there for him.

Bottom line: Be empathetic, and your teen will feel more encouraged.

Deeply demonstrating empathy through active listening will often open a door to helping your teen do the next right thing. When you do this, you are exhibiting respectful behaviors and modeling how you want your teen to treat you and others. We love God when we love others well. Letting our teen be the one to decide to take action versus being told they *have to* do something can often make a huge difference.

Just as you would with another fellow believer, we need to understand that we best encourage each other through:

1. Listening.
2. Understanding.
3. Demonstrating compassion and empathy.
4. Praying.
5. Offering a verse of encouragement.
6. Offering a life experience that demonstrates we have shared in similar sufferings.

We sometimes forget that a task we think is simple can become overwhelming to our kids simply because they've never done it before. Encouragement doesn't happen when we lecture, pull, or push. People can't be forced to take action if they are not in the right place on their journey. It is respectful to ask permission before making a suggestion to any adult in your life, and the same is true of your relationship with your teen. Doing this encourages them to take ownership.

We can start a conversation by saying, "I don't know if this means anything to you or if it would even be of help, but as I was praying for you today, God kept bringing this verse to mind. Do you mind if I share it with you?" Other door-openers for dialogue are questions like, "Are you interested in some free advice?" and "Would it help if I . . . with you while you . . . ?" "Are you open to a different perspective?" and "Do you mind if I share a thought?" are also ones you might consider employing. Softening advice and asking permission are more respectful approaches, and the Holy Spirit will open the doors to healthy dialogue if we will choose to practice respect and listen well.

What About You?

- ☐ When have you struggled with trying to encourage your tween or teen to do something important? What can you do differently next time? How will this impact your relationship?
- ☐ How do you feel about asking permission to speak suggestions or advice into your teen's life? Have you ever considered sitting with your teen as they did something they were having difficulty doing? Why or why not?
- ☐ How do you like others to speak into your life? Are you

open to them only when you ask for feedback? How has someone encouraged you to do something that required stepping outside your comfort zone? How has someone discouraged you from doing something similar?

☐ Ask your children to give you some feedback on what you can do specifically to listen and empathize better. Ask them if they feel like they can talk with you about anything without judgment. Find out if they see you as bossy, or if you ask permission to speak into their situations. Apologize for how you've hurt them in the past, and then do your best to be better at this in the future.

☐ How did that go? Share with a friend or your small group what you have learned through this dare.

Pray with us:

Lord, sometimes parenting takes so much energy. I know that my kid is smart and that the tasks I give are fairly simple, but they seem to procrastinate until I either yell or nag or—even worse, Lord—just do it myself. Help me take the time and energy to find out what the real reason is for what appears to be my child's laziness. Help me realize when my children are emotionally struggling with something. Help me encourage them to talk about their feelings and for me to talk about mine as well. Most of all, help me be willing to walk beside them when they need encouragement or a listening ear.

Your Word says that You are our refuge and strength, our ever-present help when we are in trouble. Help me not to fear, though the earth gives way and the mountains fall into the heart of the sea. Sometimes it feels like the waters roar and foam and the mountains quake with their surging in our home. Help me always remember that You are there when I cry out to You.

In Your Son's name I pray,

Amen.

Dare 15

USE HUMOR WHEN THINGS GET HOT

"There is a time for everything . . . a time to weep and a time to laugh."
—ECCLESIASTES 3:1, 4

A cheerful heart is good medicine, but a crushed spirit dries up the bones.

—PROVERBS 17:22

Adrienne sat in the driver's seat with a smile on her face as she listened to Nicole tell her story, thinking, *You go, girl. Thank You, Lord, that You are using my mistakes to help someone get it right.*

The friendship between the two women had grown in depth as Nicole's kids were becoming teenagers. Adrienne enjoyed hearing Nicole's triumphs and defeats in her parenting journey, and was grateful for the opportunity to encourage her, and sometimes offer some wisdom, along the way.

For Adrienne, the sad truth was that she had made mistakes, lots of mistakes, especially as her children kept pushing for freedom through the teenage years. Adrienne remembered being so afraid of what her children might do that she tried to seek control over every situation, just like the generations that preceded her had done. In the end, despite all her efforts, God had allowed one of her children to follow through with the very things she had feared.

Adrienne refocused her thoughts on Nicole's story.

"It is just like you said, Adrienne. I kept my cool and made something funny out of it. Here I was walking downstairs to get a tray out of the storage area, and my son and his girlfriend were lying on the couch all entwined in each other's arms! They didn't even hear me coming. I thought my heart would come out of my chest, it was pounding so hard! Oh no! My son could actually get a girl pregnant! Not that things were even close to that level, but, oh my, everything was going through my mind."

"What did you do?"

"Just like you've always told me, I couldn't give way to fear. I knew I shouldn't react too strongly and I had to think quickly, so I walked right past them over to the windows and opened them up with a laugh, saying, 'It sure is getting hot in here!' Then I told them they might want to do something else, because Cory's brother was coming down to do his homework."

"Wow! I can't believe you were able to pull that off with such ease. I would have been shaking in my boots. How did they respond?"

"You know, they were obviously embarrassed. But they handled it really well. It wasn't too long before Sidney and Cory came upstairs and asked me to take Sidney home. They both apologized in the car, and we talked about drawing boundaries around relationships. It was a really good conversation!"

"Oh, Nicole, I'm so glad you were able to do that without lashing out in fear. We sometimes forget that some of those moments are for laughter and teaching rather than condemnation. Nicole, I so appreciate you sharing your stories with me. It feels like Joel 2:25 is actually happening in my life, like God is restoring the years that the locusts have eaten. It makes me feel like God is allowing me a do-over for all the mistakes I've made. I wish I had taken Isaiah 41:13 to heart when I had teenagers: 'For I am the LORD, your God, who takes hold of your right hand and says to you, Do not fear; I will help you.'"

"Well, I've certainly got to remember that one! It is obvious that God created us to be sexual beings. Hormones are definitely raging in my house! I'm glad I can talk openly with my kids, and I sure am glad you are there to help me! I don't know what I would do without you!"

> **Bottom line: Humor teaches more than a lecture!**

For many of us, our natural tendency when we encounter our kids doing something that embarrasses or scares us is to become unhinged, heatedly pointing out what they are doing wrong and demanding an immediate change in behavior. We miss an opportunity by reacting emotionally instead of handling the situation in a self-controlled way and dealing with our teens respectfully.

When we react to our kids with forceful commands, we not only put strain on the relationship but we close down dialogue by creating defensiveness. In the heat of the battle when emotions are high, our kids' first reactions will be to go into fight-or-flight mode. Our job as parents is to avoid going down this path and, instead, to garner their attention enough to end the activity while respectfully dealing with the issue at hand. Sometimes that means diffusing the situation with an injection of humor or using a lighter tone to keep your teen from automatically putting up walls. A well-placed joke can relieve the tension and create a safer environment for you to address the bigger issue and put your child in a more relaxed frame of mind so that he can work through the conflict with you more constructively.

Knowing how to handle these kinds of issues does not come easily for many of us. That is why it is so beneficial to have an older, wiser woman who has already been down this road to walk with. A godly older woman can offer you perspective and wisdom. Treasure those women in your life.

What About You?

☐ In what type of situations have you thought the worst or overreacted to your child's actions? What did you do? Did it help or injure the relationship? Why?

☐ If your reaction caused conflict, how did you repair the relationship? If you didn't make an attempt at repair, why not?

☐ Can you think of a time when you used humor instead of reacting out of anger or fear? How did your teen respond?

☐ Think of a situation where you could have prevented a conflict from escalating had you kept your sense of humor.

☐ As your child gets older, what are some of your biggest fears? Have you and your husband talked about these? Take these concerns to God, and actively choose to trust Him with the outcomes, regardless of what they are.

☐ Do you have a Titus 2 woman or two with children older than yours walking beside you? If not, who might be some potential women you could ask? What makes them a wise choice? Contact them and ask if they would be willing to talk through a parenting issue with you, taking care to ask them to keep the discussion in confidence to protect your teen from gossip. Pray for God to confirm what they tell you. You'll know they are women of valor if they incorporate the Word into your discussions and point you back to Him.

Pray with us:

Oh, Lord,

It is such a scary world out there. Thoughts of having to potentially navigate some of those what-ifs can be overwhelming.

Help me know that You are in control and are weaving the tapestry of my children's lives. Give me the ability to quickly think on my feet when I encounter those situations that make we want to either attack or run. Show me when laughter is a good way to defuse the tension and create a teaching moment. Your Word says that You did not give me a spirit of timidity, but a spirit of power, love, and self-discipline. Remind me when these situations come up that I am to engage and teach with love and that I need to be disciplined in keeping my anger in check, knowing that nothing can happen to my children that You don't allow.

Lord, I also pray that I can find a Titus 2 woman who can speak truth into my life and give me perspective. Send someone with whom I can share my fears, my struggles, and my successes, someone who can laugh and cry with me on this parenting journey.

In Jesus' name,
Amen.

# STAY OUT OF GOD'S WAY

My dear brothers and sisters, take note of this: Everyone should be quick to listen, slow to speak and slow to become angry.

—JAMES 1:19

No temptation has overtaken you except what is common to mankind. And God is faithful; he will not let you to be tempted beyond what you can bear. But when you are tempted, he will also provide a way out so that you can endure it.

—1 CORINTHIANS 10:13

Walking into the kitchen to fix dinner, Cindy noticed her teen quickly closing the lid on his laptop. "Finished with homework?" she asked.

"Ugh . . . almost," Aaron responded, frustrated. "Something's wrong with this computer, though. I'm not able to access some of the stuff I need for my history class." With that, he grabbed his computer and went to his bedroom, books left behind.

Hmm, she thought. *Not again!* That wasn't exactly the response she had been hoping for.

Cindy was pretty happy with the small Christian school Aaron began attending a few years ago. The teachers seemed genuine, and most of the kids she had met came from good homes. She had been a little hesitant when the school decided to issue all the high school kids a laptop for their school work, but for the most part, Aaron did seem to get his homework done quicker. It was a little frustrating some days, though, especially when he couldn't access the files he needed. Most of the teachers loved the new program, and the faculty had insisted they were working out the bugs in the system and watching the computer usage. They had even blocked inappropriate website access. She just didn't understand why Aaron kept having problems with his computer.

While chopping the vegetables for dinner, Cindy kept thinking about Aaron's computer issues. Other parents she had talked to didn't seem to have nearly the number of problems with their kids' computers as Aaron did.

That night at dinner Cindy's husband offered to take a look at the computer.

"No, Dad," Aaron responded. "I think I've got it fixed. I'll let you know if I need help."

"That's fine, son, but I'm happy to take a look at it."

"No, Dad," he insisted. "I'll just have them swap it out at school if it continues to be a problem."

"You've done that three or four times in the last couple of months. Are all the kids having these kinds of problems with the computers?"

"Yeah, some of them," he responded. "They're looking into it."

The next evening, as Cindy and Tom settled down to relax in the family room, Aaron came in carrying the computer and looking distraught. "Dad, I think I need you to look at it. It won't do anything. Mr. Hammar, the tech support guy at school, said I may have to pay to replace it if I can't get it fixed. He wouldn't swap it out."

"Aaron, you haven't tried to download anything that would impact the restrictions placed on the system by the school, have you?"

"A few kids gave me some URLs and told me I should check them out. I don't think they should be a problem." He hesitated.

"Tell me more," Tom responded.

"Uh . . . Dad, they're sites you're not going to be real happy about."

"And why is that?"

"I just need them off my system, Dad." Aaron flung the words as he left the room.

Tom worked for several hours before he was finally able to access the Internet history and downloaded files. "Oh, Cindy," he gasped. "I think we have a problem. There's porn on this computer. I can't believe he's doing this! He knows how we feel about that. The school might even expel him! Where is he?"

As Tom's emotions started to escalate, Cindy took a deep breath, attempting to remember what she had learned in the parenting class they had taken at church. Then 1 Corinthians 10:13 came to mind.

"Tom, let's think through this before we react," she cautioned. "We may not have encountered this with our other kids, but let's try to walk through the situation with grace and humility. It's not about us and how we feel; it's about Aaron. Let's tell him he won't be able to take his laptop to school tomorrow because you want to work on it some more. That will give us time to pray and talk before we respond."

Her husband agreed.

Aaron seemed quiet the next morning, and when he returned home from school the next afternoon, he headed straight to his room. Cindy went on as if nothing were wrong. It was hard . . . really hard. She wanted to shake him and ask him what he thought he was doing, but she held her tongue. Instead, she fixed his favorite snack and asked him about his day. Rather than sit down to talk as they normally did while he ate, Aaron mumbled something about not being hungry as he went up to his room.

That night the story finally came tumbling out as Aaron revealed how a junior on the basketball team had borrowed his computer one day. The older student had figured out a way to get around the blocks on the system and had downloaded some pictures on several of the guys' computers after practice. Aaron had been embarrassed about it, so he hadn't wanted to talk about it, especially since he'd been struggling with the temptation to look at stuff ever since. As Aaron continued his story, tears started tumbling down Cindy's face. She grieved at his loss of innocence, but she also sensed he was aware of his mistakes and desired to make a change.

Thank You, Lord, for this trial, she sang within her heart. *Thank You that Tom and I were able to pause for a day to search for Your wisdom rather than push the issue last night. Thank You that Aaron is accepting ownership for what he has done. Thank You that we have realized this is not about us. Now help us find grace as we take this to the school. Help us think through a plan with Aaron's input on what needs to be done to address the issue.*

> Bottom line: Pause, and let God work.

Most parenting experts tell us that our biggest mistakes are often the result of not taking the time to uncover the underlying cause of misbehavior. Only addressing the behaviors and not what's going on with the heart doesn't do anything to solve the real problem. It seems easier to see these things when a child is younger, like realizing the tantrum-pitching toddler is actually just hungry. We have to put in more effort when it comes to our teens and tweens.

Many older children's behaviors are rooted in temptation or a desire to feel accepted, valued, loved, worthy, etc. If parents take a moment to pause and step back, often their kids will share what God is revealing to them and bring up the root causes themselves . . . if they feel safe enough to do so. To create this safe place where our kids feel able to open up to us, we need to model transparency about our own struggles. We have to be careful what we share, however, as we do not want to cause our kids to fear instability because of our level of transparency. Do not discuss the specifics of your marital problems or job concerns with your kids, for example, but do admit you are struggling, working on it, and expect it to get better.

Creating this safe environment takes daily work, but it is worth it. When we take a pause before responding to avoid unhealthy reactions, we give God space to work in our children and provide us with wisdom. Give yourself and your husband some grace too. Know that you aren't always going to respond the right way and that you'll be tempted to wrap up your identity in what your kids are going through. Over time you'll get better at taking your thoughts captive and focusing on the things God wants you to focus on.

What About You?

- ☐ What is your typical response when your children do something that is against your value system? Why is it important to see your children as innocent until proven guilty rather than guilty until proven innocent? How does doing that affect the relationship?
- ☐ Experts tell us that giving the benefit of the doubt is crucial to keeping a relationship healthy, yet we can't always fully trust kids' behavior. How do you best balance these two conflicting ideas?
- ☐ What safety measures are in place in your home to deal with the technology issues in our culture such as porn? Do you impose these same safeties on your own devices? How does your family talk about these things? Do you think you have established wise rules? Why or why not?
- ☐ If you are using this book in a small group, what suggestions have you heard from this dare that you could implement in your home? How will you discuss these things with your family in a way that isn't accusatory?

- ☐ If you have struggled with Internet overuse (social media or shopping addiction, pornography, etc.) come clean with your family when discussing the use of timers or filters for your devices. Many teens will self-regulate if given timers. Establish guidelines for gentle accountability with your teen, such as checking in weekly to discuss both of your timer reports.
- ☐ Write a prayer of release, based on what you sense God is revealing to you from today's dare. Be sure to confess any overreactions you've had with your children, ask for forgiveness from God (and later from them), and ask God for help in doing better at this in the future.

Pray with us:

Dear precious Father,

There are so many times I overreact to things that I find my child has done. Help me understand what is going on in my own heart. Is it fear? Is it self-condemnation that my child isn't perfect? Or is it a reaction that has been instilled since childhood and I've been trained to react as my parents might have reacted? Help me understand why I respond as I do. Also make me aware of the best way to respond in those situations so that I don't continue the pattern. If there are times I have overreacted, please bring them to mind this week, and give me the courage not only to ask for Your forgiveness but also help me bravely reengage with my child over the situation so that I can ask their forgiveness. Help me catch myself in the future so that I can parent without reacting but with humility and grace. Help me pause and take the time to pray and lift my child up to You, trusting that You are doing an amazing work in my child's heart.

In the name of Jesus who took away my sin,
Amen.

Dare 17 PRACTICE THANKFULNESS

Give thanks to the LORD, for he is good; his love endures forever.
—1 CHRONICLES 16:34

Where can I go from your Spirit? Where can I flee from your presence?
If I go up to the heavens, you are there; if I make my bed in the depths,
you are there.
—PSALM 139:7–8

Sarah could see her daughter's black-and-white polka-dot leggings as she moved beneath the hanging banners. She was eleven years old and too young to wander around the museum alone, so Sarah continued to monitor the girl's location every few seconds.

Their family was visiting the Dachau concentration camp in Munich, Germany, and it was as gray a day as they come. Rain drizzled relentlessly on this dark place in history. Two hours into the visit, despite carefully noting where her daughter was the entire time, Sarah looked up and Lizzie had disappeared.

Sarah walked ahead to the next room in the museum. Lizzie wasn't there. Sarah started to pray. She turned and ran back to the two rooms they had already walked through. Lizzie wasn't there either.

Sarah felt her heart begin to pound. She looked through the water-stained window into the grayness outside. No one was around the barracks. As if in agreement with the growing tension in Sarah's heart, the sky opened up and rain poured down in a torrent much more forcefully than before.

She went to find her two teen boys and her husband who were outside the museum theater where they'd been watching a documentary. She quickly told them what had happened and asked, the panic rising, "Have you seen her?"

They had not.

The family spread out to search. They agreed to meet back in fifteen minutes. The time came and no one had found Lizzie. Sarah had run the length of the entire museum four times. "Taking every thought captive" had never been more difficult. They were in a foreign country, and Lizzie was a beautiful young girl. The fear of her being abducted grew with each passing minute. She had been missing for over half an hour. Sarah texted a few of her friends in the States to pray. It hadn't occurred to her that it was only 6:00 a.m. back home, but her friends didn't mind and immediately began to pray—and in eight minutes, her husband found their daughter.

Thankfully, Lizzie had gone back to the front of the museum, sat down on a bench in the small information room, and waited. Sarah had checked there three times, but Lizzie had been sitting in a place where Sarah would have had to walk all the way into the room and then completely turned around to see her. She hadn't done that.

Her built-up fear masqueraded as anger when she finally saw her daughter. "How did you end up there? Why didn't you stay closer to me?"

She caught herself as she heard the words coming out of her mouth. She saw hurt register on her daughter's face. Sarah changed course—she shouldn't be angry, but thankful instead! She took a deep breath and bravely chose to be vulnerable and speak the raw real truth in her heart.

"I'm not mad at you. I'm sorry I said that. I'm so thankful you were found! I'd be devastated if anything happened to you. I love you so much; I would cry buckets of tears."

Her daughter relaxed. So did Sarah. Big breaths and a hug, and a few moments later, they were texting their friends to let them know all was well and to thank them. The family finished their tour of the museum.

The fifty-degree air and pouring rain might have been worth complaining about, especially since they were all soaked and cold, but no one did. Instead, they were all just thankful. Sarah thought of the inhabitants of the camps who had spent months and years in worse conditions, never feeling warm even on an average day. She wept for the fathers and mothers who survived the packed cattle-car train ride to the camp, only to be separated forever from their children. She knew she would never suffer this way, and neither would her kids. She was thankful her family was intact and that even though she started to "blow it" she was able to salvage the situation.

Bottom line: Challenge your anger response with gratitude and you'll respond with greater calm and real truth.

Believing that God is in control when potential harm strikes will help us get through the tough moments of parenting. We need to take the time to develop the habit of not panicking, focusing instead on life through the lens of Philippians 4:8: "Whatever is true, whatever is noble, whatever is right, whatever is pure, whatever is lovely, whatever is admirable—if anything is excellent or praiseworthy—think about such things." If we train our minds in the simpler moments, these habits will more naturally kick in when it really matters. We will find ourselves trusting God more deeply and more intentionally.

If you know where your kids are, if you have heat or air-conditioning, if you can speak out about what you believe without being beaten or thrown in jail, if you have one friend or more you can call no matter what time it is, if you have bread in your pantry, if you know you will eat tomorrow, if you have medicine, shoes, and a job, no matter how small, that pays in blessings or actual money—be thankful. And be thankful if you have kids, regardless of how imperfect your family might be. Be thankful for the positive attributes of the person you married and the kids you gave birth to. In general, be thankful at all times.

What About You?

- ☐ How have you responded when one of your kids has been extremely late or been in another situation that might cause worry? If you have responded with anger, have you thought about the love and fear that lie underneath it? What keeps many of us from giving voice to *the real truth* of our feelings, causing us instead to react with anger, as Sarah did initially when she found her daughter?

- ☐ What verses could you remind yourself of in a moment of panic if circumstances seem out of your control? If you don't know some, do a search on "comforting verses" online, and pick a few to put on a card to carry in your wallet or phone case.

- ☐ Do some research on what it means to be poor in your country; then do a little research on the Nazi concentration camps and the small amount of food the people of Dachau survived on. Do a thankfulness inventory of your life. Is it easy for you to find positives? Do you focus on what is good, or do you often complain and point out what is wrong?

- ☐ Research by Dr. Richard Wiseman shows we are happier and more content if we count our blessings from each day right before bed. Keep a gratitude notebook next to your bed. Before you go to sleep each night, write down three things you are thankful for that happened that day. If you are struggling with a relationship, devote a few nights to focus specifically on what you are thankful for in that relationship.

☐ Being thankful for the small things will help you find contentment in your own circumstances. Look around your house, and thank God for what you have that others may not.

☐ Read aloud Psalm 108:1–5, knowing that we have so much to be thankful for:

"My heart, O God, is steadfast; I will sing and make music with all my soul. Awake, harp and lyre! I will awaken the dawn. I will praise you, Lord, among the nations; I will sing of you among the peoples. For great is your love, higher than the heavens; your faithfulness reaches to the skies. Be exalted, O God, above the heavens; let your glory be over all the earth."

Pray with us:

Lord,

Help me be thankful in the little things. Most days I take so much for granted—the clothes I wear, the roof over my head, my family. Even when times of difficulty seem to engulf our family, help me see You in the midst of it, to be thankful in all things, as Your Word says.

You look down from heaven and see us. You watch me; You watch my children. There are so many times that my children are out of my sight, and I'll admit that sometimes I worry. I need to remember that You are El Roi, the God who sees. You remind me in Scripture that You sent an angel to find Hagar near a spring in the desert when she was afraid and ran away from Sarai. Help me always to call out to You when I desperately need Your intervention. Keep reminding me that You are my Shepherd and the Shepherd of my children. May I always run to You, knowing that You will protect us. May I always be thankful that You are watching over my family.

In Your precious Son's name,
Amen.

BE TRUE TO YOUR WORD

"All you need to say is simply 'Yes' or 'No'; anything beyond this comes from the evil one."

—MATTHEW 5:37

She is clothed with strength and dignity; she can laugh at the days to come.

—PROVERBS 31:25

Loretta and Jacob pulled into the driveway. Immediately Jacob scurried from the car and commanded, "Be ready in ten minutes! And I'm hungry. Make me a sandwich!"

Hmm . . .

Loretta wondered if aliens had abducted her fourteen-year-old and replaced his brain with someone else's. Her family never treated each other like that. Loretta decided not to respond while she was irritated and instead chose to wait before addressing the issue. Giving herself that time helped her stay calm.

"Thank You, Father, for this opportunity," she whispered.

Knowing that teenagers are frequently in phases of hormonal flux, she also chose not to take his behavior personally. Loretta sensed the Lord's prompting for a teachable moment, and instead of carrying out her son's request, she went upstairs, lay down on her bed, and started reading a magazine.

Jacob burst into her room. "We have to leave! We're going to be late. What are you doing? Where's my sandwich?"

Oh my. Father, help me be Your love to this man/boy.

It was time to push the reset button.

"Jacob, I love that you have all these friends and fun things to do. I usually enjoy taking you places, and I love to see you spend time with your friends. However, I have noticed that you have been increasingly bossy the last few weeks, and though I've talked to you about this a few times, you haven't changed your behavior. As a result, I'm not going to make you a sandwich, nor am I going to drive you over to your friend's house. You can go, but I won't be the one getting you there. If you want to walk, that's fine," she told him.

His mouth fell open, eyes wide. "But . . ."

Then she got up, left the room, and went out the front door to get the mail. She knew he needed to chew on what had just happened. She chose to give him space to process.

When she came back in, Jacob was waiting. "You're right, Mom. I've been really rude and bossy. I'm sorry. I haven't been respectful, and you don't deserve to be treated like that. It must make you feel like I take you for granted. I really appreciate your driving me around and stuff. Will you forgive me?"

"Of course I forgive you. Thank you for understanding how I feel. I do feel taken for granted. I don't want to feel that way in our relationship, and your apology and how you treat me in the future will impact that. Thank you," she replied.

"So can we go?" he asked.

"Honey, you can go, but like I said, I'm not going to drive you over there. Let's see how things go, and maybe tomorrow or the next day I'll feel like driving you around again."

"But you forgave me. I'm confused," Jacob replied.

"I love you and I do forgive you, but there are consequences."

Jacob eventually managed to talk his friend's mom into coming to get him, and when he returned, he was a kinder, more respectful, gentler young man.

> Bottom line: Say what you mean, mean what you say, and keep your
> commitments—this will change your relationships!

There is a line we walk daily as we interact with our children between respecting the temple of the Holy Spirit (ourselves) and serving our family. Sometimes our children don't fully understand our role in their lives, and expectations can creep in that don't lead to mature behavior. It is important that we don't allow our children to manipulate us into getting their way. Once we state that we are not going to do something, we shouldn't let them tug on our heartstrings to make us back down on our decisions. Simply let your "yes" be "yes," and your "no" be "no," without emotion. Accept their apology, but once you've stated a consequence, follow through. This will give them time to process their mistakes.

Remember, too, that it is important to develop your own relationship with God so you know how to handle the situations that present themselves to you daily. If you stay connected to God, you'll be wise to the Enemy's lie that you are a doormat when you serve. As a mom, you have the opportunity to gently teach the next generation to respectfully treat you with dignity.

What About You?

☐ Do you ever feel taken advantage of in your family? Is it by your kids or in other relationships? If so, what might you do to push the reset button and set some healthy boundaries for yourself? Remember, boundaries are for you; they aren't punishment for other people.

☐ What do you think of the way Loretta handled the situation?

☐ Notice Jacob called his friend's mom to come get him. How

would you have felt in that situation? If you saw the mom the next day and she complained about coming to pick him up, what would a healthy response—one that respected her and honored your boundary—look like?

☐ Do you have difficulty letting your "yes" be "yes" and your "no" be "no"? Explain.

☐ How do you generally react when your child makes demands of you, or are your kids considerate of your time? Do your reactions need to change? How?

☐ Is your relationship with God so close that you hear His voice when opportunities for a reset present themselves? Discuss what might need to change in order for this to happen.

Pray with us:

Heavenly Father,

I will admit that at times I have allowed my children to take advantage of my generosity. Sometimes I feel I need to always respond to my children with love, so I continue to take them places and acquiesce to their requests when, in reality, I need to be teaching them how to respect others, especially me. Lord, am I modeling self-respect in these situations? Is there something I need to be doing differently rather than always responding to my children's demands? I love that You know me, Lord. Give me strength to teach my children rather than just meet their needs.

Give me the strength and wisdom to hold fast to the bound-aries and rules I have set for my children. Help me teach my children to trust that I will do what I say I am going to do. Let them learn from me to have integrity and be true to their word.

May my prayer be from Psalm 139: "You have searched me,

LORD, *and You know me. You know when I sit and when I rise; You perceive my thoughts from afar. You discern my going out and my lying down; You are familiar with all my ways. Before a word is on my tongue, You,* LORD, *know it completely. You hem me in behind and before, and You lay Your hand upon me. Where can I go from Your Spirit? Where can I flee from Your presence? If I go up to the heavens, You are there; if I make my bed in the depths, You are there. If I rise on the wings of the dawn, if I settle on the far side of the sea, even there Your hand will guide me, Your right hand will hold me fast. For You created my inmost being; You knit me together in my mother's womb. I praise You because I am fearfully and wonderfully made; Your works are wonderful, I know that full well."*

Lord, help me respond to my children well, modeling the truth that You fearfully and wonderfully made me.

In Your Son's name,

Amen.

OFFER COMPASSION INSTEAD OF JUDGMENT

Carry each other's burdens, and in this way you will fulfill the law of Christ. If anyone thinks they are something when they are not, they deceive themselves.

—GALATIANS 6:2–3

"Do not judge, or you too will be judged. For in the same way you judge others, you will be judged, and with the measure you use, it will be measured to you."

—MATTHEW 7:1–2

S itting in the multipurpose room on Wednesday evening with a group of other parents, Barbara's mind raced. The parenting course had helped her feel connected with other parents in a comforting way. Her struggles didn't seem so large when she listened to others who were going through similar things. She listened to Marlene, the woman sitting across from her, reading aloud the scenario they were to discuss. Barbara dropped her head.

Oh, this could be our story. Please, Lord, don't let anyone suspect. I'll try to be quiet during discussion, but please don't let my emotions give way.

Barbara's daughter had recently announced that she was a lesbian. This precious girl God had finally given her after eighteen years of praying was on a path that grieved Barbara. Alisa had grown up surrounded by a family and church community who loved her deeply. God's Word had been a daily part of their home life. Barbara had prayed tenaciously for this child as she wrestled through her high school years, only to be heartbroken by Alisa's struggle with gender issues.

As Barbara read the questions in the workbook in front of her, she contemplated whether this small group of mothers was safe. Their group had been together for five weeks. Maybe it was time for her to free herself of the burden she carried. Maybe it was time to be real on a deeper level. As she debated in her mind as to whether she should share her story, someone in the group interjected into the conversation, "Well, you know what they say about gay people . . . if it is a girl, then it has to do with the relationship with the mother. If it is a boy, it must be the dad."

Barbara was crushed. *How can this person say something so cruel and uninformed? I love my daughter; we have a great relationship. I don't like what my child has chosen, but is it my fault? This woman has no idea what she is saying.* So she kept her secret to herself.

Barbara was quiet the rest of the evening. She never returned to the classroom after that.

Her daughter had been raised in a Christian home—loved, nurtured, prayed over—but when she was struggling with her choice to lead a different lifestyle, her Christian friends had walked away. Alisa's Christian friends' parents forbade their children to have anything to do with her. A young woman who was questioning, seeking answers, and looking for love in the wrong places was ostracized and rejected. She felt forced to choose the only path that was safe.

Months later, Barbara shared about her daughter with her best friend. She needed to tell someone, and she finally voiced her fears. "Why can't Christian people just love Alisa? I may not like what she does, but doesn't God call me to love her? I hate feeling judged or looked at like something is wrong with me or my parenting. Why can't people just walk beside me, holding me up in prayer, giving me a voice to talk about my daughter?"

Kate put her arm around Barbara. "I'm so sorry. I know this must hurt. I know your heart aches for a place to share what's going on. I'm sorry you got judgment when you needed compassion. Sometimes I hate that we're all at different places in the journey."

Bottom line: Choose compassion over judgment and others will feel safe.

None of us knows what choices our children might make that don't line up with our value systems. If we are experiencing the pain of a wayward child, it would be helpful to find another woman who has been there to help shoulder the burden. If we are blessed with children who are making good choices, we can choose to empathize with others' pain even when we don't understand, creating a safe haven for other women to be real and find healing.

If you read through Kings and Chronicles in the Old Testament you will learn from the kings of Judah and Israel that regardless of their parents' connection to God, sometimes their offspring will choose the opposite. "He did right in the eyes of the Lord" or "he did evil in the eyes of the Lord" is the theme that runs through these scriptures. Even God Himself had children who chose not to follow His instruction, as we see with Adam and Eve in the garden of Eden.

Yes, it is true that as parents we have the ability to influence our children. How we interact on a daily basis while they are under our roof will have an impact; however, even if we do everything right, our kids *still* have to find their own way. They still have to work out their own relationship with God. They still are going to make a ton of mistakes, learn lessons the hard way, and make decisions that might cause us to cry. In the end, we need to remember that God is ultimately in control. Maybe He is weaving a testimony in our children so that one day He can use them for His glory.

Are you ready to let go of blaming yourself or blaming others for the choices your child is making? Can you work past judgment toward others if your kids are "doing right in the sight of the Lord" while theirs are not?

What About You?

☐ How would you respond if your tween or teen were to tell you they were involved in something that was against your belief system?

☐ Do you know of any paths your children have chosen that go against your values? If so, what choices are they making? If your children are choosing other paths, what steps are you taking to build your relationship with them? What are some different options to consider that might help you in this?

☐ Nearly all parents at some point struggle with their children's choices. Have you tried to encourage a parent who might be struggling in this area? Why or why not?

☐ Does one of your children have friends who are engaging in activities you are concerned about? If so, what is your stance on your child interacting with the other kid? Is your stance based on fear or Scripture?

☐ In what way could you walk beside a struggling parent? If you have children the same age, could you link arms with your tween or teen to be a friend to the struggling child? If so, how might you do that?

☐ Did you notice that Barbara missed an opportunity to make an impact on her small group by hiding the truth about her situation? How would you respond to a parent who gently and bravely said, "It makes me so sad to hear these things. I'm currently dealing with this situation, and I'm afraid of

how you will judge me and my kid now that you know. I
need support and compassion, not judgment, and would
love this to be a place that was safe enough for me to share
the truth. If it's not, I'm probably not going to be able to
come back." Would you have the courage to speak your
truth into a group in this way?

☐ Think about when you hold back from sharing what
struggle you are going through with others. Often we are
emotional, and we may only feel safe enough to share with
one person at first, but how can we use the challenges in
our life to live out the truth that "people's lives are not their
own"[1]? What impact could talking about our struggle,
after we have processed with a safe person, have on others?
In Barbara's situation, what good could have come from
sharing her struggle with the group?

☐ Strike up a conversation with your tween or teen about their
thoughts on being gay, having sex, drinking alcohol, or
doing drugs, and listen to their opinions. Do not argue, and
know that this conversation is about hearing your child's
heart. Your job is not to convince them of your opinion but
to listen. Two days later, if necessary, you can come back
to the conversation, asking questions and interjecting your
thoughts simply to give perspective and impart biblical
truth.

☐ Read Psalm 102:1–7: "Hear my prayer, LORD; let my cry
for help come to you. Do not hide your face from me when
I am in distress. Turn your ear to me; when I call, answer
me quickly. For my days vanish like smoke; my bones burn
like glowing embers. My heart is blighted and withered like
grass; I forget to eat my food. In my distress I grown aloud
and am reduced to skin and bones. I am like a desert owl,

like an owl among the ruins. I lie awake; I have become like a bird alone on a roof."

If you are currently going through a struggle in your own parenting, know that others have experienced similar thoughts and feelings and, as this psalm shows, that you are not alone. If you are not currently struggling in a parenting difficulty, think of a friend who is hurting as they parent and try to encourage them.

Pray with us:

Dear precious Jesus,

There are so many times when I feel helpless about the choices my children make. I know in my heart that these are their choices, but I can't help but feel responsible for them. People say things that make me feel judged, like I'm a bad parent, and I admit that I sometimes believe those lies. I'll admit that my children's actions feel like they are a reflection of me and who I am. I question what I've done wrong. Help me remember that I am not responsible for the choices others make, even my children. Help me stand firm in the truth that Your steadfast love never ceases and that Your mercies never come to an end. Your mercies are new every morning. You are always faithful. Give me strength to lift my head as Your child, knowing that You are weaving my child's testimony in spite of any actions I make as a parent. Hold me as I grow through the pain.

In Jesus' name,
Amen.

 *Dare 20*   # GIVE YOUR KIDS GRACE

But since you excel in everything—in faith, in speech, in knowledge, in complete earnestness and in the love we have kindled in you—see that you also excel in this grace of giving.

—2 CORINTHIANS 8:7

Be kind and compassionate to one another, forgiving each other, just as in Christ God forgave you.

—EPHESIANS 4:32

Jolted from her silence by the interruption of the telephone, Melissa answered and heard Linda's voice on the other end. "I need your wisdom. I'm scared. Jim is out of town at a convention, and I can't get ahold of him. Jeremy is in trouble. I don't know what to do. Can you come over right away and walk me through this? Hurry, the police are expecting me."

Without thinking twice, Melissa ran across the street to console her friend. "Linda, how can I help?"

"Just help me think. I've never dealt with anything like this. The police called to tell me that Jeremy is being held in security. He was caught stealing something from a store. They want me to come right away. How can this be? Not Jeremy."

As tears streamed down Linda's face, Melissa reached for her friend's hands to help keep her from shaking. Quietly, Melissa encouraged her to sit down for a few minutes. "Linda, tell me everything you know."

"That's all I know. They just said they are holding Jeremy down at the shopping center for stealing."

"Is this something you would ever have expected from Jeremy?"

"No! Of course not!"

"Why not?" Melissa gently inquired.

"Of all my kids, Jeremy is the last one I would expect to get into trouble. He's doing great in school, almost all A's, and I really like his friends. It just doesn't make any sense. He's got money in the bank from working last summer. Why would he need to steal something?"

"Has anything been different lately?"

"No, I don't think so," she mumbled. "What would he possibly want to steal? Wait—he is getting pretty serious with his girlfriend. Surely he wouldn't be stealing, you know, something he might be too embarrassed to buy!"

As Linda's mind started heading toward unthinkable possibilities, Melissa gave her a hug and offered up a quick prayer.

"Linda, look at me. The truth here is that Jeremy is a good kid who has done a stupid thing. We've all done stupid stuff. Now it is up to you to be a strong mom for him. You can't go in there crying or getting angry. Just focus on what you know to be true. Jeremy is a great kid, and you are a strong mom. You can do this. Go be there for your son."

As she walked back to her house, Melissa knew she'd be on her knees during the next hour.

Later that evening Linda dropped by with a smile on her face. "Melissa, you were right." As she shared the details of the afternoon with the police and Jeremy, she seemed content with how the experience had turned out. "You wouldn't have believed it. As we were leaving, the police officer looked at me and told me what a great son I had. Luckily, Jeremy doesn't have to go to court, but he will have to pay a fine. He managed to redeem himself with the officer even after he did such a stupid thing. I felt sorry for him. I could tell he was really scared—and repentant. I'm glad I was there for him."

"Linda, how did you respond to Jeremy when you got there?"

"It had to have been God. I just went in and calmly asked Jeremy what happened. Even when we were walking to the car, I kept silent. I let him talk."

"Wow. What restraint."

"The crazy thing about the whole situation is that he stole a card-collection game similar to something he sold in a yard sale last summer."

"Why?"

"Seems his girlfriend's little brother was into the same card game Jeremy used to be into when he was that age. Jeremy was wishing he still had his collection to give to him. Said he was having a hard time paying for something he had practically given away in the yard sale. Jeremy remembered opening the box in the store, but the rest is a little fuzzy. When the security guard followed him into the parking lot, it was like a lightbulb came on in his head and he realized what he had done. He immediately turned around and handed the merchandise over to security."

"Oh, Linda, you've raised a good kid. It was one of those brain-freeze moments."

"I know how you've told me that the frontal lobe doesn't fully develop until between the ages of twenty-four and twenty-seven." She laughed. "I think I just experienced that today."

Bottom line: Avoid jumping to conclusions and instead ask for the full story. Then your kids will know you can be trusted.

Research shows that the brain doesn't fully develop until sometime around twenty-four in females and around twenty-seven in males. Add to that the fluctuations of the amygdala, which is the part of the brain that controls our emotions and emotional behavior, in any given situation, plus the hormone changes our children experience, and it's no wonder our tweens and teens make decisions we can hardly fathom. One of the things we need to grasp as parents is that our kids *are* going to do things that make no sense to us. The question we have to ask ourselves is, how will we respond?

One of the important things for us to do as parents is to provide a safe haven for our child to talk about what they were thinking in the moment. Most likely that will only happen if we have responded calmly many other times before and they deem us safe. If we were unable to remain calm in the moment, we need to take time to apologize for how we responded to them. Let's face it, we make mistakes too. Responding harshly or disparagingly is not the behavior Scripture espouses. We need to ask God to help us focus on what is true by getting our emotions under control. Then when we interact with our teens, they can see what maturity really looks like.

What About You?

- ☐ If you had been Jeremy's mom, how do you think you would have responded to the situation in the story?
- ☐ What things came to mind when you read Melissa's advice? Look back over Melissa's interaction with Linda before she left to go get Jeremy. What did both women do that was helpful?
- ☐ Linda's mind started thinking about all the things Jeremy could steal, which led to her worst nightmare. What do you think Linda was thinking? What did Melissa do to pull Linda out of her downward spiral?
- ☐ Who is your go-to person when your emotions are spinning out of control? If you don't have someone, why not?

☐ What effect does your go-to person have on you? Are they making suggestions based on intuition? Scripture? Experience? Their worldview?

☐ How well do you control your emotions when faced with difficult tween and teen situations that you aren't sure how to handle? What do you do well? What do you wish you could do better?

☐ Ask your teens if they feel like you would be someone they would come to when or if they got into trouble. Get specifics without becoming defensive about what you can do to become a safer place for your children.

☐ Ask your teens if you spend enough time celebrating successes with them and talking about the ordinary moments of the day, or if they feel they only hear from you when there is a problem. Take their feedback to heart. Apologize to them and to God, and repent, making the effort to do better.

☐ What steps do you need to put in place for yourself the next time your child makes a stupid choice? Are there elements of your life that are off balance, like lack of rest, disorganization, working too much, addictions, etc., that limit your ability to deal with a situation calmly and rationally, especially in an emergency?

Pray with us:

Lord, You know that my emotions can get the best of me when my children do the unthinkable. My natural tendency is to spit out words of disappointment, anger, and belittlement, or to walk away and hold back my love in retaliation for the hurt I feel. Instead, help me extend grace and compassion to my child, no matter the situation. Remind me to focus on what is true and what I know about my child. Give me strength to keep myself together during the trials. Help me see these as opportunities for growth for my child and for me. Help me to one day be able to look at these experiences with laughter as I say, "Look what God did with that situation," knowing You were in the midst of it. Help me be real enough with a few close friends so that I have support when I can't see You in the midst of disappointment.

In the holy name of Jesus,
Amen.

Dare 21   TAKE TIME TO LISTEN

"I am the good shepherd: I know my sheep and my sheep know me. . . .
My sheep listen to my voice; I know them, and they follow me."

—JOHN 10:14, 27

Marcia sat in the small chair in her bedroom with tears of frustration. She hated it when she and her husband weren't on the same page with how to handle a situation with one of the kids. She was really struggling this time not to just go ahead and do what she thought was right. Bryan traveled a good part of the week, so he wasn't as attuned to the situation as she was. She felt as if she knew Kassie inside and out, and this would be a pivotal decision that might set the tone for Kassie and her dad's relationship in years to come. In Marcia's mind, it wasn't a hill worth dying on. In Bryan's, it was.

"Lord," she cried. "You know my heart. I want to be in agreement with Bryan on this situation, but You know why I'm not. Your Word says that when I call out Your name You will hear me. I need You to hear me right now. You know my angst over this, and You know Bryan's heart as well. I know that he is a good dad. I know that he wants to follow You. But sometimes we are on totally different pages. I know that in his mind he is obeying Your Word with regard to raising these children. I know that the family he grew up in had lots of rules. My desire, Lord, is for him to make decisions based on each kid and their heart, not just a list of dos and don'ts.

You know I've tried to reason with him and it hasn't worked. What am I to do, Lord?"

Marcia waited quietly. In her brokenness she envisioned herself sitting on Jesus' lap with His arms wrapped around her.

"Speak to me, Jesus," she breathed. The longer she sat there, the more she could feel His presence. Soon she began softly singing words of adoration. As song after song flowed from her lips, she began to feel a peace within her over the situation with Kassie.

Be still and know that I am God.

"Thank You, Lord."

Bryan loves Kassie as much as you do. Give him time. You know that he values your opinion about the kids. Be still.

Even though the words weren't audible, she knew it was the Lord speaking. Being still wasn't easy for her. Marcia's typical mode of operation was to push the issue until she and Bryan ended up in an argument. This time would be different.

As she lay in bed two nights later, she and Bryan had still not spoken of the issue again. *Lord*, she prayed silently. *We only have—*

"Marcia, I've been thinking about the decision with Kassie. I know you feel strongly about how we should handle this, and I think we should do it your way. I'm still not totally convinced it's the right decision, but you do seem to be more intuitive about what's best for the kids. Go ahead and tell her yes."

"Thank you, Bryan." She paused. "I have no idea if we'll later regret this decision, but I do think that it will be a maturing opportunity for Kassie. Why don't you tell her our answer in the morning? I think she will really appreciate that she has your vote of confidence. I think it will draw the two of you closer together."

"Marcia, thanks for giving me a few days to think about it without bringing it up. I spent a lot of time praying. I felt like God was telling me that it's time to start letting go of some of the rules I grew up with."

Bottom line: Before discussing parenting struggles, start with prayer and listen for God's direction.

Many times as moms we think we know best, but we should always go to God and lay our concerns before Him, listening for His guidance. We should also listen to our husbands and what God has revealed to them. God has placed our husbands in a position of leadership in our homes, and they are responsible before God.[1] It is important that we give them opportunities to lead and respect their perspectives in the parenting process, knowing that if we work together, better decisions will be made for our children.

Remember, time can be your friend. Pushing the pause button for a day or two does several things: it allows your emotions over the situation to return to neutral, it teaches your children to plan ahead and not constantly be making last-minute requests, it honors your husband by giving him the time he needs to process how best to lead, and it allows for you both to pray.

Both you and your husband grew up in different family circumstances that can lead to disagreements as you parent. Having a united front with your children provides security and prevents kids from playing each parent against the other. All too often when kids don't get the response they want from one parent, they will go to the other one, causing conflict in the household. Sometimes the best response when a child has a request is to let them know that you need to pray about the situation and speak to their father first before you give an answer. This response will strengthen your marriage as well as your parenting skills by providing a unified front to the kids.[2]

First Peter 5:6–7 says, "Humble yourselves, therefore, under God's mighty hand, that he may lift you up in due time. Cast all your anxiety on him because he cares for you." If you cultivate a relationship with God and take time to listen for His voice in response to your needs, you will have no doubt that He is working in your life. The more you do this, the better decisions you will make as parents and the more confident you will become that God is in control of each and every situation you encounter.

What About You?

☐ Do you and your kids' dad parent as a team or are you parenting separately? What can you do to get closer to being on the same page, keeping what's best for your children as more important than your differences with their father?

☐ Are you and your husband ever on totally separate pages about a decision for your child? If so, how has this separateness created problems? What can you do to help get both of you on the same page?

☐ What would be the best way of handling decisions when your teen tries to get the answer he or she wants by pitting you against each other? Ask your husband how he would like to deal with this situation. Get on the same page about how you will handle things before it occurs. Have an honest and respectful dialogue about how you can both do better at parenting when you don't agree in a situation. Don't wait for a crisis; be proactive and establish a plan.

☐ What did you think about Marcia's time with God in the story? Have you ever had a conversation with God where you sat and listened? What happened?

☐ Sit down with God this week and be transparent with Him about your parenting concerns. Try listening rather than doing all the talking. Did you allow yourself to be vulnerable and authentic? Did you pause to listen? Why do you think it went the way it did? Don't be frustrated if it didn't go the way you hoped. Learning to wait and listen for God is a skill that takes time. Sometimes He may bring a verse to you, sometimes a thought, and other times a picture. Be open to where He leads.

Pray with us:

Heavenly Father,

I want to know You so well that I can hear Your voice. Sometimes I do all the talking in my prayers. Maybe doing this causes me to miss the things You are trying to teach me. Help me take time to listen.

When it comes to my husband, Lord, I need to remember that we are both parents of these children. Sometimes it frustrates me so very much when he thinks differently about how to respond in a given situation. Sometimes he becomes so adamant that his way is right when I feel just as strongly that my way is the better choice. Help me learn to listen to his opinion and ask him why he thinks his response is better. When I have a strong opinion that his way is not the best, help me gently encourage dialogue with him rather than get angry or do it my way anyway. Help us look to You for answers to our parenting questions and to always come to You when we have conflict. I know that my husband wants what is best for each of our children. He loves them as much as I do. Help me interact with him over crucial decisions with a gentle and quiet spirit.

In Jesus' name,
Amen.

Dare 22 COACH YOUR KIDS ON NAVIGATING CONFLICT

*What causes quarrels and what causes fights among you? Is it not this,
that your passions are at war within you?*

—JAMES 4:1 ESV

*Do nothing out of selfish ambition or vain conceit. Rather, in humility
value others above yourselves, not looking to your own interests but
each of you to the interests of the others.*

—PHILIPPIANS 2:3–4

Olivia stood at the kitchen window watching fourteen-year-old Emily interact with her slightly younger brother, Dean. She had seen them go into the backyard together after they got off the bus. After backpacks landed on the deck, both had climbed up in the treehouse that was still standing in the corner of the property. Sitting on the wooden planks, the two were in deep conversation.

Olivia had just been thinking earlier about how blessed she was by their continued friendship even as they entered the junior high years. She wished she'd had a similar companionship with her siblings growing up. As she stared, entranced by what was transpiring between them, Oliva suddenly saw Emily's face turn visibly furious. What had appeared to be a casual exchange between brother and sister suddenly turned into a fit of anger, followed by a wrestling match with fists flailing.

Olivia felt herself moving toward the door in slow motion. Just as she reached the back door, she saw Dean push Emily up against the side railing, allowing himself a little relief from his sister's continuous blows. Thankfully it was enough to stop the fight before someone fell from the six-foot-high perch.

Ordering each of her kids to their separate bedrooms, Olivia assured them they would talk about it later when cooler heads prevailed.

"Lord, I have no idea what just happened!" Olivia whispered out loud as she settled herself in a chair in her own bedroom. At least dinner was already in the crockpot, which would give her some time to sort out her thoughts. Behind closed doors she voiced her prayer. "You know what this is all about. Please help us get to the truth, and give me wisdom on how to best handle the situation. Give me Your eyes and ears to truly understand what my children are thinking. Calm my heart, and may Your glory be seen in this situation."

At the dinner table, it was obvious that neither of the kids was going to speak to the other. After dinner dishes were put away, Olivia walked into Dean's room.

"Is now a good time to talk about this afternoon?"

"I guess so. I just don't get Emily anymore. She's changing. And not in a good way."

"How so?"

"She seems to want a boyfriend so badly that she'll do just about anything to get one."

"Is there something specific you want to share?"

"Not really. What she did was not what our family is about. In her mind it's all about her and not about us."

"Can you tell me more? Like why she got so angry?"

"I told her that what she did was impacting me as well and that I thought what she did was wrong. She didn't like what I had to say."

"I'm glad you love your sister enough to speak truth to her. I hope you were kind and respectful in the way you spoke to her. Something sure seemed to set her off."

Olivia wondered from his lack of response if he had been a little too blunt while dishing out truth.

"I'm not sure how we are going to resolve this, but I'll get back to you after I've had a chance to talk to Emily."

Later that evening, Olivia approached her daughter. "Emily, do you have a minute to talk?"

"I guess so."

"Do you want to tell me what was going on out there in the treehouse this afternoon?"

"Mom, I just got so angry at Dean. He has no right to tell me what I should and shouldn't do. It's none of his business."

"Oh?"

"Well, it *is* none of his business. I can make my own decisions, and he needs to stay out of it."

"Do you want to tell me what Dean is so upset about?" she gently asked.

"I'm sure he already told you everything."

"Actually, he didn't. He told me you did something today that he thought was wrong and it had an impact on him. Do you want to tell me what happened?"

"Not really."

"Would I have been upset at what you did?"

"Probably."

"Do you think it was right to go after Dean the way you did?"

"You would say it wasn't. I just hate having a younger brother tell me what I shouldn't be doing."

"Ah. Yes. Younger brothers. I remember those days. My younger brother, you know, Uncle Dan? He always seemed to know what was best for me. At least in his opinion. Sometimes he was right. Sometimes not." Olivia paused. "Emily, family is about 'we.' We want what is best for you, and it sounds like that was what Dean was trying to convey to you. I'm not sure if he did it kindly or respectfully, because I wasn't there. Regardless, at least listen to him. He may be right. And having a brother who loves you enough to confront you, even if it is done poorly, is worth a lot. Any of our actions might have the potential to impact others. You can't avoid that, no matter what it is you want to do. Does that make sense?"

Silence from Emily.

Olivia continued, "Emily, your dad and I want you to become the person God created you to be. Obviously I don't know the details of what happened today, and I'm choosing not to ask, but I'm thinking maybe Dean confronted you because he cares for you as his sister and wants the best for you. Life isn't all about you. Your entire life you will have to make choices, but know that those decisions will more often than not impact others."

Continued silence.

"Let's plan to go to lunch on Saturday and talk about what happened today. Maybe I can help you sort through what you are feeling and why you did what you did. In the meantime, I'm hoping that you will pray and work through your anger with Dean. If you had a friend who reacted to you the way you reacted to him, you might see things from a different perspective."

Again, silence.

"Emily, I love you no matter what. Your dad does too. Dean loves you a lot. He wouldn't have said anything to you about today if he didn't. I want to listen to your side of things and be there to help you and your brother work through whatever this is if either of you want that. We all make mistakes. Learning to own up to them and talk about them with those who love you will help you in the future. Right now, you just need to know we are always going to be here for you, no matter what."

After hugging an icy Emily, Olivia left the bedroom. She headed toward Dean's room to say good night.

"Dean, I spoke to Emily and encouraged her to think about things from your perspective. I also told her I don't know if you were kind or respectful in how you handled this, so you might want to think about things from her point of view as well before you two continue the discussion. If you need help working through this, I'm available. I'll be praying for the two of you. I love you."

The next morning Olivia overheard Emily knocking on Dean's bedroom door. "Can I come in?" she asked him.

"Sure," came the reply.

When the kids came downstairs for breakfast, they were smiling at each other. Olivia thanked God for intervening and seeming to help the siblings work through their conflict.

"You two get things worked out?" she inquired.

They smiled and nodded, mouths filled with pancakes.

"Good. I'm glad. I'm proud of you both. It takes courage to work through difficulties, but it is worth doing. Your relationship will be better because you did." Olivia smiled back at them.

Bottom line: If we ask questions, we will help our teens see more than their side of a conflict.

Parenting through sibling conflicts can be difficult. In some of our homes, we moms feel like the standard uniform should be one of referee stripes or a coach's jersey. Sometimes we want to know the details so we can set the standard in our homes, as well as make sure our children understand what they did wrong and why it matters. Other times we want to pretend conflict didn't occur at all and avoid all aspects of addressing it. Sometimes just encouraging our children by asking a question instead of giving them an order allows them to own their mistakes and solve their problems without feeling that we are micromanaging every situation. It can also be helpful to set up a time later to work through the details if your child chooses to share them. This usually takes the emotion out of the situation. For some kids, the time between the event and the discussion can be twenty minutes, while for others it can take days to work through their emotions. Guiding them in a way that creates a sense of empathy will deepen the emotional intelligence they will need throughout life. Remember, the important piece is that our children need to see that we are in this life together and we both want the same thing—for them to be the best at who God created them to be.

What About You?

- ☐ How do you handle situations in your home when your children have sibling squabbles?
- ☐ By the time your kids are tweens and teens, parents should be coaching rather than telling their kids what to do. When they are little, we usually know all the details, but as they get older, we may never know the particulars of all their squabbles. How does that make you feel as a parent? Have you moved from refereeing to coaching? Why or why not?
- ☐ Sometimes as parents we want to know everything that is going on with our kids. How does Philippians 2:3–4 at the beginning of this dare speak to you on this subject?
- ☐ Sometimes when our kids fight, we don't necessarily seek to understand the passion within them. What was Dean's passion in the story? What about Emily's?
- ☐ Imagine you are Olivia and want to have a good conversation with Emily on Saturday. What would your goal be? In other words, what do you want the outcome of the conversation to be? How would you avoid causing her

to be defensive and instead open up to you? How would you begin the conversation to discuss what happened with her brother?

☐ If you are studying this book in a group, take turns role-playing how the Saturday conversation between Olivia and Emily would start. Those who are watching should coach "Olivia" when her conversation takes a wrong turn.

☐ Write a prayer to God about your family. Ask Him to reveal to you the relationships that need to be strengthened. What might your role be in helping to be a bridge between your children or possibly even between a child and your spouse? Are there conversations you might need to initiate? Are there areas where you need forgiveness because your behavior or actions might be affecting the connection?

Pray with us:

Father God,

I know that in many ways my job as a mom is to be a relationship architect in our home. When I see strife and conflict not being resolved well, it is so difficult to watch. I'll admit sometimes I don't handle it well either. Show me how to be a bridge in our home to provide opportunities for relationships to be strengthened. Give me the words that will encourage positive interaction. When my kids or husband find fault with each other, help me defuse their frustrations with the other person and encourage forgiveness and restoration. Give me confidence and skills that will nurture positive relationships in a way that will help our home be a reflection of You.

In the power of the name of Jesus,
Amen.

Dare 23 — PARENT AHEAD

For we are God's handiwork, created in Christ Jesus to do good works, which God prepared in advance for us to do.

—EPHESIANS 2:10

Don't let anyone look down on you because you are young, but set an example for the believers in speech, in conduct, in love, in faith and in purity.

—1 TIMOTHY 4:12

Lauren's young eyes met her mom's and she smiled, handing her mother the tissues.

"I told you the movie would make you cry!" Lauren's bell-like laughter bounced around the room.

Emotion leaked out of the corners of Joanne's eyes again. She couldn't get enough of these moments. Joy overflowed.

They hugged.

"Mom, I just love this weekend. It's the best ever," Lauren beamed.

Joanne agreed.

While the men in their family spent the weekend in a cabin in the woods, estrogen prevailed in their home as mom and daughter walked through Family Life Ministry's Passport2Purity program. Through the discussion of familiar topics, the sharing of CDs, and the forging of new commitments, they engaged each other in the beginnings of a dialogue that would hopefully continue throughout Lauren's growing years and impact her future in a positive way. Joanne shared some really personal things about herself (age appropriate, of course), and Lauren did the same. Boys, men, sex, periods, makeup, music, movies, magazines, social media, you name it, the two talked about it. They shared stories about hurts and hopes. They both talked about mistakes and struggles, and Joanne conveyed her dreams for her daughter's future with the man she might marry someday.

The realities of sexual pressure and temptation became real when Lauren shared stories of girls her age who were already sexually active. Joanne realized she would have a lot of praying to do during the coming years.

They talked a lot about God, prayed together, and discussed challenges Lauren would face as she grew older. The entire weekend was one to remember for the both of them.

Bottom line: Link arms early in the culture battle, and your kids will have a more solid foundation on which to stand in the fight.

If you aren't familiar with the materials from Family Life, they are some of the best tools out there for helping young daughters and sons navigate the difficult waters of peer and sexual pressures. Keeping the dialogue open without judgment or emotional reaction helps tweens and teens know that you will be safe to talk to when peer pressure becomes overwhelming or they are struggling with sexual temptation.

We have to remember that we live in a very sexualized culture. When your tweens and teens encounter situations at school, at the movies, or at the mall, talk about them from a biblical perspective. Share the struggles you or others (without names) have endured. Pray with your children openly about temptations and the choices that they or their friends encounter.

Giving kids a combination of the following in a healthy home can help equip them early on to deal with life and its inevitable pressures:

- A strong sense of identity (being uniquely created for the glory of God)
- A relationship with Christ (modeled by the parents as well)
- Family members who are there for them (a sense of belonging and acceptance at home)
- Knowing they are safe and their circumstances aren't going to change
- Feeling like they can achieve at something

It's never too late to create an environment where kids know in advance what is coming for their next stage of life. Doing so allows them to walk through the waters with more self-confidence and less pushback toward their parents. Let them know you are always there to walk beside them even if they make mistakes, trusting God on the journey.

What About You?

- ☐ If you were to ask your child if you are safe to talk with, what do you think he would say? Why? If he were to say yes, what have you done to create that safety? If you think he would say no, what steps could you take to change his response?
- ☐ On a scale of 1 to 5, with 1 being "needs lots of improvement" and 5 being "doing really well," how do you think your home stacks up against the list of characteristics for a healthy home for your teen?

- A strong sense of identity (being uniquely created for the glory of God)
- A relationship with Christ (modeled by the parents as well)
- Family members who are there for them (a sense of belonging and acceptance at home)
- Knowing they are safe and their circumstances aren't going to change
- Feeling like they can achieve at something

☐ Looking at the list in the above question, where do you need to focus some attention? Why? How are you going to do that?

☐ Identify struggles that you think your children might encounter and at what age. Put together a plan that will allow for preemptive parenting, and set dates for when you will begin the conversations. Consider weekends like Family Life's Passport2Purity for you and your kids, and encourage your husband to take your sons for a weekend for the male course from Family Life. If you are late in talking about these issues with your kids, apologize and work out a plan for dealing with the challenges you face as a family swimming against the culture together.

☐ Have transparent (but age-appropriate) conversations with your kids about your own struggles. They already know you aren't perfect, and it's prideful to pretend you don't make mistakes. It puts walls up between you and breeds resentment.

☐ If you aren't already, add praying for your kids and their friends to your daily prayers. Invite your husband to join you. Keep a journal for each child to give to them when they are older. Even if your child is nineteen, he'll appreciate knowing what you prayed for him and seeing how God answered those prayers.

☐ Add admiration to your daily communication repertoire. Start with an intensive one-per-day note campaign and hide a note in your child's lunch, shoe, outside her backpack, or some other easily accessible place. Pointing out a character strength supported by a specific example of how your child exhibited it will reach your child's heart. For example: "Kris, your compassion for others makes God and me smile. I love how you helped your little sister with her homework last night." After doing this daily for a week, put a reminder on your calendar, and continue this practice once a week until your child leaves home. You can also do this via text, but notes will be kept longer.

Pray with us:

Abba Father,

You are so good. Psalm 36 says, "Your love, O LORD, reaches to the heavens, Your faithfulness to the skies. Your righteousness is like the mighty mountains, Your justice like the great deep. O LORD, You preserve both man and beast. How priceless is Your unfailing love! Both high and low among men find refuge in the shadow of Your wings." Thank You for the opportunity to teach my children Your ways, even in the midst of the world's tainted views. Help me do it well—to show them Your precepts and faithfulness. Help me paint a picture of Your ways in a manner that helps them want to embrace Your goodness and choose life over potential death. Help me also convey my love to them in such a way that they come to know that regardless of their mistakes, I will show them the mercy and grace that I receive from You.

In Jesus' name,
Amen.

Dare 24 TALK YOUR KIDS THROUGH DISAPPOINTMENT

Better is a poor man who walks his integrity than a rich man who is crooked in his ways.

—PROVERBS 28:6 ESV

Show me your ways, LORD, teach me your paths. Guide me in your truth and teach me, for you are God my Savior, and my hope is in you all day long.

—PSALM 25:4–5

Valerie sat on the edge of her bed with the door shut, tears starting to roll down her cheeks. She couldn't believe how ungrateful her fifteen-year-old was! Trying to convince herself that it was just fatigue, she curled up and let herself fall into a fitful sleep. While she slept, she seemed to be subconsciously wrestling with the demons from her day. There was little rest that night.

As Valerie later shared her story over a cappuccino with her friend Hillary the next day, she was still struggling to understand what she was doing wrong.

"It was Jordan's fifteenth birthday. I just wanted it to be special. When I asked her what she wanted for her birthday, she gave me a list of five things. I bought four out of the five, but all I heard about was what I didn't buy! I feel like I'm raising an ungrateful, spoiled brat," she muttered. "What am I doing wrong?"

"Valerie, if you don't mind, I'd like to ask you some questions.

Did God give Jordan to you for you to make her happy or to teach her His ways?"

"Oh . . ."

"Is your role to make everything in her life perfect or to teach her that she won't always get what she wants in life and to learn how to deal with the disappointment?"

"Okay, I think I'm getting where you are going. I should talk to her about her disappointment and help her find ways of coping with it."

"That's it."

"But . . . she was in such a foul mood!"

"Valerie, I think it would help you a lot to read Ecclesiastes 3:1–8,[1] and specifically verses 1 and 7. The Bible says, 'There is a time for everything, and a season for every activity under the heavens . . . a time to be silent and a time to speak.'

"Timing in relationships is so important," she continued. "Give her time to work through her emotions. Wait until she is calm and ready to talk. If one of you starts getting too emotional, your job is to close the conversation to protect the relationship with something like 'I think we need a break from each other right now. When our emotions are under control, we'll talk some more.' Then you can initiate the conversation again when both of you are calm and ready to talk."

"But how do I do that?"

"What if you said something like, 'I know you were disappointed that you didn't get _____ for your birthday. Tell me why that was the most important gift I could have given you,' and then calmly dialogue about it. Let her see you understand why she wanted it, and then ask her if she's interested in knowing why you chose the gifts you gave her and why you didn't purchase that particular one."

"That makes sense, but I know that won't be easy for me. I'm not always patient enough to work through the problem. I just want it to go away. I don't want her to feel disappointed, and I don't want to feel bad because I didn't make her happy. But I know I need to have a long-term approach and take the time to teach her how to be content."

Bottom line: Teaching your kids contentment will help them find happiness.

Parenting tweens and teens is tough these days. They are bombarded by marketing and what their friends have, and sometimes have a difficult time learning that parents can't provide everything they want. Sometimes parents, and especially us moms, feel inadequate when we can't fulfill our kids' desires. After all, we just want life to go smoothly and for them to be happy. Unfortunately, this thinking is too often wrapped up in materialism. Our job is not to fulfill our kids' dreams in order to make them happy; our role is to teach them to be content and grateful so they can handle disappointment when things do not go their way or they don't get what they want.

Consider taking your kids on a mission trip once a year so they can get a good look at how most of the world actually lives. Sponsor a child from Compassion International, and have your child build a relationship with him or her. Focusing on others will help your kids be more grateful and put their own struggles in perspective.

Realize, also, that most of the growth in the Bible came to people in the midst of suffering. If we try to prevent any suffering for our kids (and often our definitions of what constitutes true suffering may be very different from theirs), we are standing in the way of their growth.

What About You?

☐ How do you typically respond when your kids are unhappy?
☐ Think of a time when you had to say no to your child. How

did it make you feel? Was it difficult to say no? Did you give them something in return, sort of like a plea bargain, to ease the pain?

☐ What type of attitude does your teen typically display about the things you provide? How do they act when they don't get what they want?

☐ How do you respond to your teen's attitude? Do you reinforce positive behavior by letting them know that you appreciate their understanding of your role as a parent? How do you handle their negative behavior?

☐ What are you modeling for them with regard to the above? Are you content with what you have, or are you seeking more and better, complaining about what is wrong with your circumstances, clothing, appliances, etc.? For the next three months, each night before you go to bed, thank God for your circumstances and something specific He has given you. At the same time, place a ban on complaints from your own lips. Refuse to complain or communicate dissatisfaction with material possessions. Wear a hair tie or rubber band around your wrist, and snap it each time you find yourself giving voice to or thinking a negative, critical, or complaining thought.

☐ Hillary suggested Valerie reflect on Ecclesiastes 3:7 whenever Jordan got emotional and Valerie needed wisdom on when to talk to her daughter. Was there a time when you wished someone had given you some time to process your emotions instead of plowing ahead in poor timing? If so, what happened? Hillary also coached Valerie by giving her specific dialogue with Jordan to help her understand her feelings better. What did she do specifically? What do you think would be effective in this approach?

☐ How can you let your child know that your job is to help them become healthy adults rather than make them happy?

Pray with us:

Lord, I know it is natural for us to want our children to be happy. Their happiness or unhappiness affects my joy and my mood. But in those times of disappointment, open my eyes to what Your desire is in the moment. Help me look at each situation as a way to instill character traits in my children rather than just focusing on what will make them happy. Give me opportunities to begin dialogue with my children that will help them mature in ways that lead to healthy responses to disappointment. Help me not to own my child's emotional immaturity in a way that makes me feel like I need to take personal responsibility for it. Create in me a clean heart that renews my spirit to one of holiness rather than happiness.
In the holy name of Jesus,
Amen.

Dare 25 DROP THE COMPARISONS

Each one should test their own actions. Then they can take pride in themselves alone, without comparing themselves to someone else, for each one should carry their own load.

—GALATIANS 6:4–5

Fathers [and mothers], do not exasperate your children; instead, bring them up in the training and instruction of the Lord.

—EPHESIANS 6:4

This morning Crystal found herself sitting at a local restaurant with a woman she had just met. A couple of days prior, Lana, the mother of one of her son's friends, had called her and asked her to have coffee. "I just need someone to talk with," Lana had explained. "I understand my son, Jamal, has been to your house a couple of times to see your son, Michael. I don't know what to do with Jamal, and I thought maybe you could give me some advice."

Always open to listening to another mom, Crystal agreed to meet.

Lana started pouring out her heart even before they ordered. "Your family is one of the few I know of with both a mom and dad," she muttered behind a look of disbelief. Crystal could see that Lana really needed someone to talk to, and she hoped she would be able to give some comfort and share some insight to this clearly struggling mom.

After giving Crystal a few details about their home life and her recent divorce from Jamal's father, Lana soon launched into the real reason she had asked Crystal to meet.

"I just don't know what to do. I don't know how to get my fifteen-year-old on the right track," she blubbered. "At his age, I was on the honor roll in school, playing a sport every season, and working twenty hours a week. Jamal's grades are awful, and he just got suspended from the football team because he wasn't making it to practice on time. Not only that, but I've been trying to get him to look for a part-time job for the last six months. He won't even try! Getting him up on Saturday mornings to mow the lawn and do his chores is next to impossible. Without his dad living at home anymore, I have to depend on Jamal to help out around the house, but he's just not pulling his weight. I do everything I can to be his friend and do what he asks me to do, but I just don't understand . . ."

After listening for over an hour, Crystal was finally able to pull Lana into the present. "Lana," she ventured, "you've done a great job at giving me a glimpse of what you are up against. It must be really hard being a single parent and trying to work while raising two kids. It sounds like you want Jamal to work harder to reach his potential. I can certainly understand that. Sometimes it's hard to motivate our kids. Would you mind if I gave you a different perspective?"

Lana nodded.

"I'm sure it has to be difficult for Jamal without his dad in his everyday life. That's a lot for any kid to handle, especially for someone who is almost a man. I wonder if life isn't a little different from when you and I were kids. Sometimes school is difficult for kids these days. There is so much pressure to succeed. Add to that your desire for him to play football and work a part-time job. Do you think that all those activities combined might possibly be too much for him? I know you were able to handle all of that in high school, which is awesome, but I'm betting that not all your peers were able to be successful with such a heavy load. This might not be the case, but do you think Jamal could be feeling the pressure of so many things that he's choosing not to focus on any of them?"

Lana sat in absolute silence for a moment. "I guess I never thought of that."

"What if you sat down with him and tried to find out what he's thinking about his future? Maybe the two of you could come up with a plan that he can and wants to manage."

"Perhaps I am putting too much pressure on him. Thanks, Crystal. I'll sit down with him tomorrow and try to have the conversation."

As Crystal lay awake that night talking with God about her conversation with Lana, a still, small voice seemed to speak. *You may be pressuring your children too, Crystal. Are your hopes for them realistic? Is anyone in your family bucking the system you set into place?*

> Bottom line: Stay focused on the unique design of each child and their circumstances and you'll resist the temptation to compare.

Instead of looking back to your childhood or at other children, your parenting focus should be on your child and developing a relationship that will help him discover who God designed him to be, not who you expect him to be.

No matter what stage of life our kids are in, our expectations are usually based on where we were at that age or where we think our friends' kids are in the journey. Early in this book, we asked you to deal with your expectations for your kids. There is a difference between hoping for what is good and having unhealthy expectations in a relationship. We're addressing this again now because we all experience a constant struggle between laying those expectations down and then picking them back up again.

Whether we want to admit it or not, all of us have dreams, hopes, and expectations for our children—and we need to be continually aware of whether what we are doing is healthy or putting undue amounts of performance pressure on our kids. We dream of free college tuition, so we set them on a course for athletic or academic scholarships. We expect our children to mature and live productive lives. We dream of fun times with grandchildren who live close by.

Expectations can be a two-edged sword. They can help our children grow and mature, knowing there is a goal to work toward, but expectations can also crush a child's spirit and hinder their growth if they are unachievable for that particular child. In the hurry-up world that we live in, sometimes we forget that things we were able to accomplish in our youth might not be the same for our tween or teen. It is also important that we treat each of our children individually regarding our expectations. "Train up a child in the way he should go"[1] actually means to train him according to the way he is bent—meaning that we need to ask God for wisdom regarding where we actually set the bar for each child.

What About You?

- ☐ What is the difference between healthy hopes and dreams for your child and pressuring expectations? Where do you see yourself having expectations? Where in your upbringing and current surroundings do your expectations come from? Where do your dreams and hopes for each child come from?
- ☐ When you have parenting struggles, do you seek advice from others? If so, do you listen well and remain open to input? Are the people you share with those who can provide wise advice? Why or why not? What do you sense God leading you to do in this area?
- ☐ What expectations do you have for your child that seem

to exasperate him or her? Are those expectations realistic? Should they be modified?

☐ Discuss the expectations you are letting go of with your child. If you are exceptionally brave, ask your tween or teen to hold you accountable for letting these go. (Know that you might have to graciously eat humble pie when your child gives you feedback.)

Pray with us:

Dear gracious Father,

How many times do I not do the things You want me to do? Yet in my sin I put wrongful expectations on others that strain our relationships. Sometimes it is as simple as wanting a family member to put something away or wanting them to take notice of how I am feeling in a given situation. When it comes to friends, I might just want a phone call that I could easily make myself, but in my selfishness I expect them to call me. When they don't, I'm hurt.

Lord, as my children grow older, when I feel expectation frustration well up within me, help me recognize whether the desire is selfish or an opportunity to teach my child a necessary skill that will make life easier when they reach adulthood. Help me choose to see the good in people even when they don't always meet my desires. Help me see their hearts, not just their actions or inaction. I know this journey is about me. Sometimes it is easier to blame others rather than look within myself. Just as Your Word says, search my heart, O God, and know my heart; test me and know my anxious thoughts. See if there is any offensive way in me, and lead me in the way everlasting,

In the precious name of Jesus,
Amen.

Dare 26 INVITE THEIR FRIENDS IN

Do not be misled: "Bad company corrupts good character."
—1 CORINTHIANS 15:33

"Then neither do I condemn you," Jesus declared. "Go now and leave your life of sin."
—JOHN 8:11

Dana couldn't believe the kids who dropped her son off after school. As she watched the car pull into the drive, the black-haired, pierced teens glared back at her. Angry-sounding music she didn't recognize polluted the air as her son got out of the car, waved, and shut the door. His cool smile quickly faded to a dark frown when he saw her watching from the window.

"What?" he demanded when he walked in the house.

"Who are those kids?" Dana asked.

"Friends," he said, shrugging and then rounding the corner to head upstairs to his bedroom.

"Yes, but who?" she asked, trying to keep up with him.

"Nobody," he sighed back, slamming the door to his room.

What has gotten into him? She worried that the fighting between her and her husband had become too much for Kyle. She knew divorce was hard on kids and that fighting was even worse, but she didn't know what to do to fix things. She and her husband were in counseling and things seemed to be improving a little, but just when she had a bit of hope for her marriage, she realized her son was slipping away.

She knocked on his door later that night.

"Yeah?" he said.

"Can I come in?" she asked.

"I guess."

"So, what's going on with us? I know things have been hard the last year, but I'm wondering how we got here?" she began.

"I don't know what you mean." He eyed her warily.

"A few years ago you were running track, laughing, and going fishing with us. You had different friends. Now . . . I just don't know. Are you comfortable with how things are going?"

"You know, you only talk to me when I'm not getting good grades. You're only interested in me when there's a problem. You expect me to get into trouble, so . . . whatever. As for my friends, they accept me for who I am. Yeah, we get in trouble sometimes, but it's nothing major and I'm going to get yelled at anyway. Might as well have some fun. Why do you suddenly care? Did you run out of things to yell at Dad about?"

He looked angry. Hurt. Eyes slit, jaw clenched, he stared at her.

She sat, chewing on his words. Thinking and praying.

"Are you saying you feel like I don't have anything but low expectations for you?" She paused. "That I think poorly of you?"

He looked at her quizzically. "You might actually get it."

Reality bit hard into her heart. "I'm sorry," she said.

"What?" he asked.

"You're right. I've been too tough on you. I've forgotten that you aren't the things that happen to you or the things you do. I've not treated you well, and I'm sorry," she replied.

He stared.

"I want to listen to you better, okay? I want to understand the things you deal with more. It sounds like I can start with how you

135

feel. What I think I heard you say was that the only time I talk to you is when you are in trouble or something's not going well. I think there might be some truth to that. And it's wrong of me, so I want to work on that."

His face softened.

"Why don't we have your new friends and their parents over for dinner this weekend?" she asked.

His eyes widened. "I'm not sure that's such a good idea."

"Well, you think about it. They are welcome here. I'd also like to spend some time with you once a week, just the two of us, maybe a coffee date?" she said.

He agreed.

In the days to come, they started going for coffee together weekly. Over time, she noticed that as she listened to him and was less judgmental and critical, his attitude improved. Slowly. She still held him accountable to the rules and he was grounded a few times, but still, she listened to him more and their relationship improved.

He never did follow up on the dinner invitation, but as the days passed, Dana noticed Kyle hanging out with one of the newer kids at school. This one he did invite into the house. And he even stayed for dinner a few times.

"I like your new friend, Kyle," Dana began one night.

"Yeah, we have a lot in common," he said.

She sighed with relief. It seemed like God had found a way to help her carefully navigate the waters without causing rebellion or damaging their relationship. She knew it didn't always go this way, and she knew it was important to continue to seek God's wisdom to know each step and be aware of how sensitive her son was. She was thankful God had revealed to her the small moments to gently speak a hard truth or ask a question. She had added lots of affirmation and encouragement to her parenting repertoire, and even though progress was slow and time-consuming, things were improving.

> Bottom line: Make sure your teens feel accepted by you, and then you'll be able to positively impact them.

Kids want to feel like they belong. If we don't listen to them, they won't feel known or accepted at home. That's when the questionable crowd becomes attractive. When you start noticing your tween's and teen's attitudes and their friends take a turn for the worst, begin the dialogue.

Be careful not to condemn but simply note (without emotion) the changes you are seeing. Lean into the relationship by investing time in doing fun things together. It may not be coffee, but most teens spell *love* "t-i-m-e" and "f-o-o-d." Ask them about their friends, what they like about them, why they enjoy hanging around them. Invite their friends into your home. This is where you have the opportunity to influence. If they hesitate at the invitation, it helps your child think more deeply about their choices. Most of all, give them time to replace their attitudes and friends without demanding immediate change. Teens need to be able to try on new behaviors to discover who God made them to be. Listen to your kids and to God. You'll know what to do and when to do it, and you'll have better relationships within your family.

What About You?

☐ Take a moment to look at your communication and time with your kids. Is most of it related to tasks, activities, or problems? Relationship expert Dr. John Gottman says that healthy marriages have a 20:1 positives to negatives communication ratio. That means for every negative interaction, there are twenty positives. Even during conflict, the ratio is 5:1. Consider what you are modeling in your marriage and in your interactions with your kids. Collect data on your interactions during an average week, and see how you measure up. Ask God to help you do better, and continue pointing out what you see your children doing right. Do this with your spouse as well, and your children will have an even higher likelihood of one day having their own healthy marriage.

☐ Invest quality time intentionally with each of your children and your husband every day. Be sure you are spending time listening and interacting with them about their lives. If you haven't created enough margin in your life to be able to do this well yet, get out your paring knife and go after your schedule.

☐ Review how often you are touching your children. Both young men and women need physical affection; if they do not get it at home, they often find it elsewhere, sometimes inappropriately. Start now hugging and tussling with each of your kids daily, but respect their requests to stop. Having a phrase like "that's enough" that will immediately be honored helps them set healthy boundaries and have control over their own bodies. Be affectionate with your children with hugs and neck and back scratches and rubs, and do the same with your husband. Ask for hugs from them too.

Pray with us:

Gracious Father,

Only You know how my child really feels and what she will seek in terms of relationship. It was so much easier to supervise who she was hanging out with when she was younger. Now that my child has more and more time unsupervised, I don't always know who is influencing her. I know nothing about the other

kids' home lives or parents. Help me to not be fearful of the inter-
actions my child has with some of these kids, but help me build
such a safe connection with my child when she is at home that she
ultimately knows who she is and whose she is. Help me to not nag
my child about her friends but be an encourager of healthy choices
in relationships, pointing out the obvious in a nonthreatening
way. May my character be so Christ-focused that as an adult she
will want me to be her friend as well as her mother.

In the precious name of Jesus I pray,
Amen.

Dare 27 SEPARATE YOUR IDENTITY

Whatever you do, work at it with all your heart, as working for the Lord, not for human masters, since you know that you will receive an inheritance from the Lord as a reward. It is the Lord Christ you are serving.

—Colossians 3:23–24

But you are a chosen people, a royal priesthood, a holy nation, God's special possession, that you may declare the praises of him who called you out of darkness into his wonderful light.

—1 Peter 2:9

On the way home from practice, Nate looked over at Sally and said, "Mom, I don't want to swim this summer. I'm done."

"Nate, you've always loved swimming. You've broken several meet records. Your coach says you have the ability to make it to the top. Why would you give that up?"

"It's boring. I just don't want to do it anymore."

"Nate, remember that swim meet when you were in the lead and then ended up in fourth place? What did the coach tell you?"

"I know, Mom. He said to go for the wall, and don't look side to side," he mumbled.

"Is that what you are doing? Are you going for the wall or looking side to side here? The coach keeps telling you you're one of the best. We all see it. Why would you give that up?"

The volume of Nate's voice filled the car.

"This isn't about looking at anything but me, Mom. It's about me. I spend every day after school in the water, and then the weekends are taken up with swim meets. I've done it for five years. I want to do something different. You can't make me keep doing this. I'm quitting."

Nate's dad, Don, spoke up. "Of course you aren't quitting the swim team, son. We've invested a lot of money into this, and you have the potential for a college scholarship. Your coach told us we would be crazy to let you quit now. No way should you be thinking of quitting," he lectured. "Here's what we'll do. I know that practice starts at 6:30 a.m. this summer. I'll go with you. We'll take a thermos of hot chocolate. We'll do it together, son."

The chilly summer mornings continued. Day after day, Nate and Don got up early to go to practice. Each morning Nate came home looking miserable.

Sally shared what was going on with a few of her friends.

"Of course you can't let him quit. He's a critical member of the team."

"I wish my son had Nate's talent. You would be stupid to let him quit."

"The team needs you too! You're a great help. What would they do without you?"

"We'll really miss you!"

And the comments were the same everywhere she turned.

As Sally spent time alone with God, though, she sensed Him saying something different. *What is the goal? Is getting a free ride to college more important than your relationship with Nate? Why do you want him to continue to swim when he doesn't want to? Is this about what others are telling you is best for your son? Are you reluctant for him to give it up because of the friendships you have formed with the other swim moms and because you enjoy the meets and all the other activities? Are your plans for him more important than Mine?*

As Sally contemplated the questions that were spinning in her head, she felt a peace that it was time to let the swim team go. "Guess I need to talk to Don," she lamented. "I need his support. Lord, if this is the right decision, give me Your words to change his mind."

Then she got up and searched out her husband.

"Don, I know you would like Nate to continue swimming. So would I. But I think we should look at the big picture. You know how Coach always told Nate to go for the wall and not look side to side? What is the wall for us in this? Is it a scholarship or a good relationship with our son that will last a lifetime? I think I have been looking side to side too much," Sally continued. "I've been asking everyone else's opinion rather than figuring out what the real wall is. Would you do me a favor and spend some time asking God what the goal is, and then let's talk?"

"Sally, I agree with you. I've been praying every morning while Nate is in the water. He's lost his enthusiasm, and I think we should consider letting him stop swimming. But there is more to this than just Nate," Don cautiously ventured. "I'm worried about you too. These other swim moms have become your friends. Will you be okay to see those relationships change and maybe end?"

> Bottom line: Keep your identity out of your kids' activities, and you will be able to make better choices in family relationships.

Sometimes our kids get involved in activities, and we just assume they will continue year after year. For some, it becomes the focal point the family plans life around. We become team mom, head carpools, and attend all the events. Soon, part of our identity becomes entangled with this gifting we see in our child. When the child is ready to disengage, sometimes we've invested so much time, money, and energy that we're afraid to let go. We're afraid they will regret the decision later. We're saddened to lose our dream of what we thought the future would look like.

There are lots of good activities for our kids to be involved in, but most important are the ones that will help us reach the ultimate goal of relationship. As moms we need to make sure our lives are structured in a healthy way so that our kids' activities don't become our identities as well.

What About You?

- ☐ What activities are your tweens and teens involved in that are creating conflict in your home?
- ☐ What changes need to be made that might bring more balance to your home life so that there is more quality family time?
- ☐ As you look at your life as a mom, how embroiled are you in your child's outside activities? Is it a healthy or unhealthy balance? Are there any of your child's activities that would feel like a personal loss to you if they wanted to quit?
- ☐ What expectations do you have for a college scholarship for your child? Is it realistic? Is your child as invested in achieving it as you are?
- ☐ Are the activities your kids are involved in based on their desires or yours? When is the last time you checked in with them about this?
- ☐ Have a conversation with your tweens and teens about their passions for school, sports, and other activities. What do they really enjoy or have time for? Are there outside activities that put too much pressure on them? This is an opportunity for you to listen.
- ☐ Write a prayer asking God to reveal to you whether your

home is out of balance with regard to activities, sports, or possibly even church work. Ask Him to show you anything that might be on your own personal schedule that needs to be added or removed for this season in your life.

Pray with us:

Gracious Lord,

Thank You for the opportunities that my children have to become involved in healthy activities. I want to provide those for my children, but I also want to do it in a manner that is pleasing to You and strengthens our family. Help me recognize when my identity is wrapped up in my child's activity. Show me when my desires don't align themselves with my child's wishes or Your desires. Most of all, help me listen to my child's heart about what activities he wants to pursue, but also help my husband and me look at the activity in relation to the overarching goals that we have for our family. My desire is for us to become a family that gets direction from You and is brave enough to say no even when the culture says we have to do it all. If someone sees our family's calendar, I pray that they would see Jesus in the middle of everything we choose to do. Show us the way, Lord.

In the name of Jesus,
Amen.

AVOID THE BLAME GAME

"Do not judge, and you will not be judged. Do not condemn, and you will not be condemned. Forgive, and you will be forgiven."

—LUKE 6:37

M om! He took my balloon!" she yelled.

"Mom! She's driving me nuts with it! Can't she just stop?" he responded.

Karen found it interesting that her children's accusations were flying at each other, although they were both speaking to her. She walked into the room where the skirmish loudly played out and observed the two siblings hurling angry words.

"If he'd just stop being so rude all the time—"

"She needs to just *stop*. I don't want to listen to her. I want to read my book—"

"You should play with me!"

"You should go away!"

"*Mom!*" In stereo, no less.

Oh, the drama.

"Okay, so both of you are angry, and both of you are blaming the other. This stops now. Let's stop throwing gasoline on the fire here," Karen began.

"But she started it!"

"That's not true—he started it!"

"I am not interested in who started it. I am putting an end to it. Whichever of you is the more mature will love first," she said.

Silence.

"I love you both dearly," Karen stated gently, making eye contact with both children. "The two of you are going to have each other for your whole lives. God has given you to each other to help you learn how to resolve conflict and develop healthy relationships so that your marriages and work relationships are wonderful. Now is when you practice how to do those things. That means hurling insults is unacceptable. That means blaming each other is wrong. You are both wrong. You need to apologize for what you have done that is hurtful, ask forgiveness, and then we can work through the issue. And, like I said, the more mature one of you will love first. Let me know if you need my help."

She turned, walked into the kitchen, and waited. Thankfully, she had intervened before the conflict had risen to a stage where feelings were deeply hurt and needed to be processed at a high level—that would have taken a ton of time, active listening, reflecting back to the other, coaching, etc.

"I'm sorry I made the balloon scream in your ear. Will you forgive me?"

"Yes. I'm sorry I yelled at you. Will you forgive me?"

"Yes. Okay, so let's work through the problem. The way I see it is . . . ," her daughter began, holding the plastic stick that meant it was her turn to talk. When she was finished stating her case, she handed the stick to her brother. The two siblings worked through their problem, only needing a few resets by Mom.

Bottom line: Teach your kids to respectfully resolve conflict, and they will develop skills to last a lifetime.

When teaching your kids to resolve conflict respectfully, focus on avoiding the blame game. In the thousands of marriages we've interacted with over the years at Greater Impact, we have found that all people are focused on the other person's behavior to some degree. From Adam in the garden (the original blamer—"that woman You gave me . . ."—blaming both Eve and God in one sentence!) to the children and married couples of today, we are a culture of relinquished responsibility, focusing on others' shortcomings instead of focusing on what we can directly impact: our own behavior and choices. Sometimes we expect our children to respond with adult behaviors, blaming kids for being kids, instead of accepting our role as coach. We know we're doing this if we find ourselves attributing our behavior to them. "He made me angry" or "her emotional vomiting wound me up" are excuses for our own lack of adult behavior.

From what we've seen, as long as individuals in a family stay focused on blame, the relationships don't improve. The world reinforces this. We end up serving the Enemy instead of God when we judge, blame, and absolve ourselves of our part in the difficulties.

It's never too late to learn how to dialogue respectfully. If your family has a firm foundation of friendship, this is easier to do. Whatever your kids' ages, teach them how to respectfully talk through conflict instead of avoiding it or being hurtful to each other. They'll have better life skills as a result.

What About You?

- ☐ How do you handle conflict in your own life? Is your method something you would want your kids to use as well? Why or why not?
- ☐ What role does blame have in your home? Take several moments and ask God to reveal what is true in this area. How have you participated in blaming others?
- ☐ Realize that blaming is sinful behavior—it is judgment, criticism, and condemnation. There is no condemnation

in Christ, and it is not our job to judge, but rather God's. Some Christians justify judging others by misunderstanding the difference between discernment and judgment. How have you participated in these sins?

☐ Confess to God your sin in this area, asking Him (and others) for forgiveness, and then ask Him for help obeying Him. Change your behavior. Note that this does *not* mean that you condone negative behaviors, but rather that you do not get emotionally wrapped up in others' actions.

☐ How do you help your kids navigate disagreement? Do you have enough skill in this department to model it well and then coach others?

☐ Ask God to help you be a better coach in navigating conflict healthily so that you can help your kids be quick to listen, slow to speak, and even slower to become angry.

Pray with us:

Father,

Far too often I get caught up in what I want rather than looking at what my child or even my spouse wants—and then it goes badly. Help me build relationship rather than fight for my own way. When my children get into conflict, help me coach them. Show me how to help them resolve situations well by teaching them to listen, to hear, to give sincere apologies, and to have non-emotional discussions. Help me view each conflict as an opportunity to learn the skills for becoming more emotionally connected. Father, I confess I am often nervous when conflict occurs and don't know what to do. Please give me growth in this area, and take away my fear so I can both model for and coach my children in having healthy discussions that honor You. Keep me from being a blaming parent. Help me not to blame others for the way things are but rather help everyone, including myself, move forward in ways that bring You glory, Lord.

In Jesus' name I pray,
Amen.

 *Dare 29* RESPOND WITH CALM

But the Lord is faithful, and he will strengthen you and protect you from the evil one.

—2 Thessalonians 3:3

"When you pass through the waters, I will be with you; and through the rivers, they shall not overwhelm you; when you walk through fire you shall not be burned, and the flame shall not consume you."

—Isaiah 43:2 esv

Synda and Eric sat in the family room in tears. "Mom, I really am trying not to do it again," Eric said. "I just can't seem to help myself."

Synda reached over to give Eric a hug. "I know you are trying. Let's talk about what you were thinking and feeling this time," she replied. She sat next to him and just listened as he unloaded his current pressures.

Self-harm had become a way of escape for Eric. He struggled with understanding his emotions and tended not to know how to soothe himself when he was stressed. The end of the semester was in two weeks, and reports and projects were all coming due, not to mention studying for finals. Synda knew Eric felt the pressure to do as well as his older siblings had in school, a weight he had put on himself.

Eric tried to put his feelings into words as Synda listened to him. Eventually he revealed his breaking point this time.

"So you feel like you are trapped, as if you are a pressure cooker just needing to get rid of the building stress," she said.

"Yeah. That's it. I can't stop thinking about it. When I have too much going on, it's the only thing I can think about, and then doing it, well, it just helps. I'm sorry, Mom."

"Oh, honey. I know you're trying to stop. I know you want to. It *is* hard. I'm glad you trust me with this. I'm so sorry you're struggling. How can I pray for you?"

He shared his heart with his mom, and she felt like she was walking on sacred ground.

As their discussion started winding down, Synda wanted to pour truth into Eric. "Eric, I know I've told you this before, but I need to say it again. You really are precious to us and to God. I want to encourage you to use this time to discover who God made you to be and not try to compete with your brother and sister. Grades don't define who you are. Perfection isn't the goal. The other thing you need to remind yourself of, son, is that your body is the temple of the Holy Spirit. When we know Him, we can ask the Holy Spirit to help when we are really struggling. He'll help you focus on something else and give you peace if you tap into His strength. Can I pray with you?"

After the two prayed together, Synda went into the kitchen to begin cooking dinner. "Thank You, Lord, for my sweet time together with Eric. He is precious to You. Strengthen him and me in this trial."

As Synda began chopping the vegetables, her mind wandered to Eric's friend, Chris, who had also been cutting. She wondered how his family was doing. She knew that the minute Chris's mom had discovered what was going on she had panicked.

"Thank You, Lord, for helping me stay calm in the midst of this crisis, and please help me do the right thing." She continued,

"Thank You for the opportunity to connect with Eric on a new level, and thank You for the progress he seems to be making."

Bottom Line: Choose to be calm, and your kids will have greater trust in you.

With every generation there seems to come a new addiction craze. Media makes it even more available to this generation. With only a few strokes on a keyboard, video and pictures of self-harm, pornography, and a host of other images are brought to life behind closed doors. The likelihood of your child being caught up in the curiosity of trying something is almost inevitable. How you handle the situation when it rears its ugly head can make a huge difference in your relationship with your child and with helping him curb the potentially addictive behavior.

Shaunti Feldhahn has written an excellent book that examines empirical data and brings light to much of what teens really think. In *For Parents Only*, Shaunti reveals some of her research results and lets us know that our highly emotional responses, *even about good things*, can make our teens shy away from trusting us with both good news and bad.[1] It is important to remember that in difficult parenting dilemmas, unless we are dealing with life and death, it is better to gradually increase the amount of intervention rather than push the panic button before we know all the facts about what we are encountering.

When you are a parent with a child in dangerous circumstances, sometimes you just want to beat the walls, argue with God over the things you can't change, and scream at the top of your lungs. You also tend to swing into hypervigilant mode, trying to watch every move your child makes so he won't do it again. Know that even if you do need to scream at God, He can handle it. Pour out your fears, your frustrations, and your questions to Him. Focus on scriptures that will give you peace. He hears our every prayer. Trust Him with the uncertainties of life. God is faithful, even when we can't see it in the midst of our circumstances. If we seek Him, then we can calmly address the situation, knowing He will walk beside us every step of the way.

Your support for your child is crucial in every step of this process.

What About You?

☐ What parenting situations have you encountered that have caused fear? How did you respond? Looking back, would you have responded differently? Why or why not?

☐ Are you a person who can respond calmly in a difficult situation, or do you typically bring in the cavalry to get the situation fixed immediately? What do you think about the idea of pausing to calmly evaluate the situation first? How can you think about this concept when you are in crisis mode with one of your children?

☐ What parenting situation has caused you to trust God most? How did this event grow your faith? What good has come out of that situation? Revisit this situation with your husband, asking him what he learned and how it grew him. Share your own growth with him. Have the same dialogue with the child involved, focusing on the growth and positive outcome.

☐ In the story, Synda was thanking God through the trial. Have you ever been able to do that? Why do you think you responded to God the way you did? Does that need to change for the future? Elaborate.

☐ Looking at the situations you are currently dealing with in your family, how can you see God at work? What possible positive outcome could there be that can provide you with hope? If you have trouble seeing hope at the moment, ask God to reveal some to you.

☐ How has God's faithfulness impacted you and your family? What does His past faithfulness indicate for your present circumstances?

☐ Do a word search at www.BibleStudyTools.com on "faithfulness," and pray some of these verses back to God. Write the ones that resonate deeply with you on a 3 x 5 card, and put it where you will see it daily.

Pray with us:

Mighty God,

Sometimes it seems as though I am walking through the valley of the shadow of death. Just like Psalm 23 says, I know that I need to remember to fear no evil, because You are with me. My children mean so much to me, and I shudder to think something could happen to them. Lord, I know You are always with me and give me comfort. May I always hold fast the confession of my hope without wavering, because I know it is You who promised and You are faithful. The things we encounter as a family teach us to depend on You. Help me not to give way to fear. Help me cling to You, knowing that You work everything together for our good. Help me respond to difficult situations with a sense of calm and peace that only comes from You.

In Jesus Christ's name,
Amen.

Dare 30 — REMOVE THE MASK

"For I am the LORD your God who takes hold of your right hand and says to you, Do not fear; I will help you."

—ISAIAH 41:13

Therefore, there is now no condemnation for those who are in Christ Jesus.

—ROMANS 8:1

Carry each other's burdens, and in this way you will fulfill the law of Christ.

—GALATIANS 6:2

Plastering a fake smile on her face, Tonya joined her Thursday morning small group. She had been in this Bible study of more than fifty women for a couple of years, but the leader had decided to change things up two weeks earlier, placing everyone in random small groups. Of course Tonya had ended up in a group with mostly people she didn't know.

Ugh! I'm not even sure I want to be here, she thought to herself. *With the way I'm feeling today, though, maybe being in this new group is a good thing. Maybe it will be easier to wear a fake smile with these women rather than share the raw feelings that come with being an inept mother. Today I can pretend.*

Isn't that what you always do? She heard the small voice from somewhere in her head. *No one knows who you really are anyway.*

Tonya sighed. *Guess I'm getting pretty good at playing the imposter. No one in this church would want to have anything to do with the real me, especially if they knew what was going on in our home.*

As the morning progressed, the women started sharing. Tonya was amazed at the depth of pain Carrie talked about as she told how her husband had left her and their three sons. Tonya found it unbelievable that she was not crying, not angry, not bitter. Carrie seemed at peace.

Wow, the strength of this woman.

Laura was the next to speak. "Pray for my twenty-two-year-old daughter. The guy she is living with has recently been diagnosed with . . ." Tonya stopped listening.

Oh my! I can't believe she just said that out loud! A guy her daughter is living with? Whoa!

Carrie comforted Laura as Tonya wondered how much she and Laura might be able to relate to each other. They both had daughters who seemed to be struggling.

Tonya's turn came around and just as she started to share a little about her wonderful family, her cell phone started to vibrate. She ignored it.

Tonya continued her story; the cell phone continued to vibrate. She attempted to ignore it again.

By the third time, Tonya mumbled, "I better take this. One of my teens is home sick today."

Tonya didn't recognize the number, but as she heard the other voice on the phone, her fear came rushing to the forefront of her mind. Quickly she left the room so she could talk in private.

"I just wanted to call to make sure you are home," the voice echoed from the other end. Tonya was shocked. It was her daughter's boyfriend's mother. *How did she get my number?* Tonya wasn't exactly thrilled that her daughter was dating this woman's son. She had lots of concerns . . . no, major concerns.

"Well, uh, no, I'm not. Tamara, is there a problem?"

"I think you should be home if you can. I'm at work, but I just found out that both of our kids are home sick today. I thought they might be up to something."

"Thanks for letting me know. I'll head home now," Tonya muttered as tears started falling uncontrollably. She headed back to her group to get her purse and keys. The ladies were praying—for Tonya!

As Tonya quietly sat down to reach her purse, they all looked up with expectancy. Tonya didn't have a chance to hide. She was too emotional to even think about putting her mask back on. It was the moment of truth, so she shared. Really shared. Her thoughts. Her pain. Her ineptness as a mother. And her most recent concerns.

As tears streamed down her face, tissues were placed into Tonya's shaking hands. Several women were crying with her—especially Laura. Laura put her arms around Tonya and began praying as the others joined in. Calm began to replace her churning stomach. Peace began to fill her mind.

"You need to go now, sweetie," they chorused. "We'll be praying. See you next week."

Tonya prayed all the way home, bracing herself for what she might find. As she entered the house, all was quiet. She was tiptoeing upstairs as her daughter walked out of her room.

"Did you go somewhere?" she mumbled, wiping sleep from her eyes.

"I went to Bible study."

"Oh, I just woke up. I really feel awful," she sniffled.

"Did you know that Brad was home sick today?" Tonya asked.

"No," her daughter replied groggily. "How do you know?"

Later, as Tonya replayed the events of the day on her knees, it occurred to her that she was living her life in fear. Fear of what her kids were doing, fear of their choices, fear of what people might think—of her kids, of her. Honestly, she was afraid of being judged as a parent. Which was why she wore the mask. But she had seen today that she didn't need to, that there was grace and even strength that could be gained from walking through things hand in hand with other parents.

> Bottom line: Bravely choose vulnerability with others, and you will create connection.

We speak to women daily who live behind the mask. If truth be known, we are sometimes our own worst enemy. We cast judgement upon ourselves when our children disappoint us or embarrass us. There is something within us that says we're at fault for the way our children behave. Why is it that we feel responsible for our children's actions? Are they not sinners like everyone else? Will God hold us or them responsible for their choices?

Most of the women we talk with have felt judged by others. Sometimes that judgement has been handed down from previous generations who expected perfection in all things. At other times it is from fellow Christians who have embraced the idea that they have to be perfect to be accepted, so they lift themselves up by pouring judgment on those around them.

Not every choice our children make (whether good or bad) can be traced back to our parenting. Our fear is rooted in the lies of the Enemy. We'd encourage you to find other women who have had parenting struggles. If they are real, then you can be assured there will be safety in taking off your mask. When you have processed your pain, we dare you to choose to live bravely, sharing your stories of how God's brought you through difficulties, because there are many women living alone behind the mask.

What About You?

☐ How comfortable are you sharing your parenting woes in a small group of believers? Why? What is the purpose of the body of Christ? See Galatians 6:2.[1]

☐ What happens in relationships when you choose to keep difficulties private? How do you get in God's way by not revealing what He has done?

☐ Is there ever a time when putting on the mask is a good thing?

☐ Do you have people with whom you feel safe to share your parenting issues? If so, think about their ages, the ages of their children, etc. What makes these people safe?

☐ Are you a safe person for others to share with, or do you give advice and try to solve other people's problems without being asked? How quickly do you judge others when they are struggling? What could you do to make yourself available for other parents?

☐ What fears are you dealing with now in your parenting? Can you be brave enough to unpack those fears with a close friend and take them to the Lord in prayer right now?

☐ Have you sensed that God has a ministry for you that you are hiding from? Ask God if the area in which you are struggling is an area He plans to birth ministry out of. If He says yes, and if your ministry is in marriage and family, feel free to contact us. Our purpose at Greater Impact is to equip others to do the ministry He has called them to do. We serve families all over the world who are making an impact in their neck of the woods.

Pray with us:

Dear heavenly Father,

I will admit there are times that I feel shame at my child's actions. I don't want anyone to know the things my child has done or how I've responded as a parent. Fear grips me as I wonder what others might be thinking or judging about my parenting. I don't want anyone to look at my child in a negative way, so I pull back in silence into my own shell of protection. Everywhere I look others seem to have it all together. Other kids seem to be so perfect. I know that is just a lie from the Enemy, and it keeps me from being vulnerable and real with others. Lord, help me see the lie for what it is—a chasm that keeps me disconnected from others because of fear.

Lord, I do desire friendship—deep, connecting relationships—but it is so scary to reveal my shortcomings or the imperfections of my child. Help me be brave. You designed me for connection, so my prayer is that You will put someone in my path whom I can feel safe with. Help me recognize that person because of her willingness to take off the mask. Help me trust You with this burden of shame. Help me remember that You created us for relationship and in You is where I need to put my trust.

In Jesus' name,
Amen.

Dare 31   DEAL WITH THE PERSON BEFORE THE ISSUE

Let your conversation be always full of grace, seasoned with salt, so that you may know how to answer everyone.

—COLOSSIANS 4:6

Therefore each of you must put off falsehood and speak truthfully to your neighbor, for we are all members of one body.

—EPHESIANS 4:25

The one who gets wisdom loves life; the one who cherishes understanding will soon prosper.

—PROVERBS 19:8

Clara listened as her daughter, Abby, droned on and on about how she didn't understand her and how she "never" let her do the things she wanted to do.

Clara started to feel a little miffed. She'd spent a good chunk of her day driving Abby to the many activities she wanted to be involved in. She regularly stayed up late at night to pick her up from theater practices and performances. The girl seldom, if ever, thanked her mom for these things and instead complained.

Frequently.

"I love you, and I'm rather tired after a long week, so I'm going to take a break from this conversation for a while. I want to finish it, but I am starting to get emotional, and that's not going to be at all helpful," she said, turning and leaving the girl's bedroom.

Clara went to her own room and realized she expected too much from this young girl. She wanted her daughter to like her, but it wasn't time for that yet. She had to stick with the parenting for now.

She'd set a boundary and decided she was done arguing with emotional teenagers. Today she respected herself by leaving the conversation, and she respected Abby by not emotionally vomiting on her or arguing with her about how good she had it. Clara had made a habit of dwelling on the things she loved about her family members as she went to bed every night. Abby obviously had not been doing the same.

After some time passed, Clara decided she was calm enough to resume the talk with her daughter and went back to the girl's room. Abby was lying on her bed, reading a history book.

"Got a minute?" Clara asked.

"Sure, what?" Abby inquired, setting down the book.

"I could be wrong here, but I'm guessing you feel like I don't listen to you very well, right? A lot of your friends have cool phones, expensive shoes and clothes, and more privileges."

"Yeah, everyone has all these things, and you won't let me have them. I don't get it," the girl replied. "You always have some lecture for me about why I'm wrong. It's, like, why bother telling you how I feel? You don't listen. And if you won't listen about this, why would you listen about something else? Something that really mattered?"

Ouch. But truth.

Even though her daughter had an uninformed and privileged opinion of what she should and shouldn't have, she had just shared the bigger issue at play. *Thank You, God, for this moment.*

"Abby, you know, you are right—I haven't listened to you well about a lot of things. I want to do better at that. I'm guessing it makes you feel unimportant when I don't hear you out, right?"

"Yeah, like you just want me to be someone else, like what I think and feel isn't good enough, like my opinions don't matter to you. Like I don't matter to you," she said, looking away.

Clara walked over to the bed and sat down next to her daughter. She took her hand and looked her in the eyes. "Honey, what I hear you saying is that you feel like when I disagree with you, I'm discounting what you think and feel, and it makes you feel like you don't matter. Is that right?"

Abby nodded.

Clara continued, "I just hate it that you feel that way. I'm sorry you feel like you don't matter to me. I don't want you to, so I'll work on being a better listener," Clara said. "Will you forgive me for not listening well and give me another chance?"

"Sure, Mom," the girl replied, smiling.

"Good. Thanks. So if you see me not listening again—or, I should say, *when* you see me not listening again, because I'm not perfect—you need to let me know, okay? Can you say something like, 'Mom, you know when we talked about listening? I'm not feeling heard right now.' Do you think you could do that?"

"Yeah. I can do that."

"Awesome. So tell me what is important to you about having a cell phone," Clara began.

"Well, I feel like when I go places, I'm such a mooch. Everyone else has a phone, and I'm the only one who doesn't have one. So when I need to be picked up from somewhere, I always have to borrow a phone. It's really embarrassing," Abby explained.

"Tell me more about that," Clara replied.

"Well, there's not much more. It's just I hate having to borrow my friends' phones. I don't understand why you won't get me my own phone," she said.

"So your biggest issue is feeling like you are always borrowing and you don't like having to do that? Is that it?" Clara asked.

"Yeah, and I'm also, like, the only one who doesn't have one," Abby continued. "Everyone has these cool smartphones, and I don't have anything."

"So are you worried you won't fit in, maybe even that people won't like you because of that?" Clara asked.

"Yeah, it's just really awkward," Abby replied.

"I remember feeling like I was the odd one out when I was about your age." Clara went on to share a story about how her friends in school had made fun of the old coat she had to wear because her parents weren't as wealthy as some of the other kids' parents. "Is that similar to how you are feeling?"

"Well, kinda. It's not so much at school, though. Usually it's at dance class or at theater. The girls seem so put together, so perfect, and I feel awkward around them. And then I have to borrow their phones, and it's just, I don't know . . ."

A lightbulb went on in Clara's head. "Has anyone complained about loaning you their phone?"

Abby shook her head. "No."

"But you're concerned they might?"

The girl pressed her lips together and nodded her head. "Yes."

"Abby, aren't those girls all older than you are?" Clara inquired.

"Yeah, I'm the youngest one there. Everyone is at least two years older than I am." She frowned.

"Abby, I could be wrong about this, but I wonder if the fact that they are all older is what is putting this pressure on you in the first place. You know how you have so many more privileges now than you did two years ago? How you have more freedoms than Kayra next door, who is just a few years younger than you?"

"Yeah, Kayra can't stay up as late. It's so frustrating—her mom makes her go to bed before 10:00 p.m.!" Abby said.

"Right now, but a few years can make a big difference. I'm really proud of you for the way you interact with the older girls, and I'm sure it feels good that some of them invite you to do things with them," Clara said. "You act really mature for your age, so I'm not surprised."

"I've been told that," Abby said, smiling. "So, can I get a phone?"

"Yes, but not this year," Clara said, smiling back. "When you are older. And you may have to pay for part of it if you want something like what those girls have. Your dad and I will be putting Net Nanny on it too, just so you know."

Abby smiled. "Okay, I guess."

"I know you still didn't get the answer you were hoping for, but do you feel better about how this conversation went?" Clara asked.

"Yeah, I feel like you listened to me. I wish I could have the phone, but I get it. And you didn't, like, get all mad; you listened and totally got how I was feeling," she replied.

"Good. Let's do more of this." Clara hugged her daughter, smiled, and left the room.

> Bottom line: Deal with the person first; deal with the problem second. This will result in dealing with both more appropriately.

Trying to address the issue or problem first can often cause conflict, especially when a disagreement is involved. One of the things we forget when dealing with someone who presents an issue to us is that the person is not the issue. The person is a precious and important creation of God's, and we need to treat them as such.

Respecting our kids means that we listen and take to heart the feedback they give us, understanding that there may be truth in it. Part of respect and love is responding to other people's needs in relationships. A humble heart will help us be able to do this; pride will get in the way. Humility builds relationship, and pride puts up barriers.

Being open to being wrong and being able to receive feedback from others are signs of humility, which is one of the things God wants from us. When we behave like this, we create safety for our kids and increase the level of trust they have in us. If we argue, debate, and make our kids feel as though they are wrong more than they feel their opinions are respected and heard, they will not trust us with the little or big things that matter in their lives, which is the opposite of what we want relationally with them now or in the long term.

What About You?

☐ It's easy to get confused about what should be dealt with in a given situation, and our tendency is to try to solve the problem first. But by focusing on making our kids feel safe and heard first, we can then regain lost trust enough to work through problems. Ask the people you live with if they feel like you really listen to their concerns and opinions or whether you discount and argue with them. Pray before doing this that they would be truthful. Make this a safe experience by starting with, "I am just checking in on my listening skills. I promise I'm not going to be hurt or angry by anything you say. I just want to know what's true." Then listen and ask follow-up questions like, "Can you tell me more about that?" and "How can I improve?"

☐ Do a verse search on listening in the Bible. What does God have to say about listening?

☐ Do you easily receive feedback from others, or do you become defensive? Ask God to reveal to you the opportunities to become more humble. Seek forgiveness from those you have injured with your defensiveness about their expression of concerns or relational needs.

☐ Make a commitment to yourself and God that you will deal with the person first and the issue second. Ask for His help in doing so.

Pray with us:

Lord, You are such a great listener. I can pour out my praise or sorrow, and I know that You hear me. Help me listen well, especially to my children. Sometimes I get lost in the whining. I get impatient. I have stuff to do and don't want to wallow in my children's list of things they want or need from me. How many opportunities have I missed to connect with my children? How many times have I not had time or not asked the right question to really understand their heart's cry? Forgive me. Help me listen with my heart so that I won't miss the important things in their world.

And, Lord, please help me create healthy, respectful relationships with myself and others. Help me set boundaries for my own behaviors and respect the boundaries they set for themselves. Help me receive feedback and apologize with empathy and emotion when I hurt someone—even if I didn't mean to do so. My lack of intention does not negate the fact that they are injured and in need of healing. I can help them do that by earnestly apologizing, empathizing deeply, and treating them as a valued treasure of God's, whom I've also hurt.

God, please humble me. May the pride in me be gone. I trust You with this.

It's in Jesus' name I pray,
Amen.

Dare 32 RESPECTFULLY CONSIDER YOUR KIDS' REQUESTS

"My command is this: Love each other as I have loved you. Greater love has no one than this: to lay down one's life for one's friends. You are my friends if you do what I command."

—JOHN 15:12–14

"Mom, can I get a tattoo? It's a really big deal. All the guys on the squad have one."

The dreaded words.

Nicole wanted to say to her seventeen-year-old son, "No way!" Typical parental thoughts coursed through her mind. *You'll be scarred for life! What will people think? I won't be able to stand looking at you with that thing.*

Somehow, though, in the course of the conversation, she managed to keep her cool. Maybe it was because he had so calmly asked the question. Maybe it was because she knew he couldn't get one without her signature since he was underage. Maybe it was because she realized she was in a position of power.

Later, Todd and Nicole spoke about the situation, wondering how they should approach it without alienating their son. First, they agreed that they did not want him to get the tattoo. Yes, they could issue a dictatorial response, but was it a hill worth dying on? Was it something that their son would hold against them in years to come? Would the decision potentially set a precedent that might impact their other children? These were some of the heavy questions they were beginning to tackle in their parenting journey.

Nicole knew what some of her Christian friends would be thinking if she told them. "What? You even considered saying yes? You must be out of your mind!"

As Todd and Nicole began seeking God for guidance, they started researching.

Ugh! It would have been so much easier if God had just said, "Thou shalt not get a tattoo," Nicole thought as she sent a question to her pastor via e-mail and surfed the Internet for information about tattoos, the Bible, and potential health risks.

Meanwhile, Todd set off to discuss the situation with friends who had already been down this path, hoping to get perspective.

They continued to discuss the topic with their son during this time, not making it an issue but showing sincere concern about what was best for him. He had his opinion; Todd and Nicole had theirs. But the dialogue remained cordial and became similar to one they might have had with an adult friend.

Todd and Nicole agreed to give their son a decision a few weeks after their family returned from vacation. That would give them some fun connecting time before they gave him their "no."

As the family enjoyed the beach together, Todd and Nicole agreed that their son was really maturing well. For the most part he seemed to be making good decisions. How badly would their decision about the tattoo impact their relationship when they said no?

And then Nicole and Todd did the unbelievable, the unthinkable, the "whatever possessed us to do this" thing—they went to visit a tattoo parlor!

It was actually quite by accident. While hanging around the dock when the kids were off doing water sports, they saw it: a tattoo parlor on the corner within walking distance. Knowing there was absolutely no way anyone would recognize them, they went in to look at tattoo designs. As they walked into the shop, Nicole kept thinking, *Father, forgive me. I know not what I am doing!*

Standing there among several employees with more color on their skin than she had in her wardrobe, Nicole sheepishly asked prices and told the girl behind the counter what they were considering for their seventeen-year-old. The girl immediately brought the owner to come speak with them.

As they explained their dilemma, Nicole asked, "What would you say if this was your kid?" She had no idea what possessed her to ask the artist such a stupid question, but he looked old enough to possibly be a dad. *Maybe he has kids of his own?* she thought skeptically.

Surprise of all surprises, he responded, "You're the first person to ever come in here to ask me that. There's no way I'd let a kid of mine get a tattoo until they're at least twenty-five, especially a male. Their body changes too much with muscle growth that skews the artwork. They also haven't figured out who they are and what is important to them yet. If it were my kid, I'd say no."

Shock resonated within her as she and Todd left. Speechless but absolutely delighted, they laughed their way out of the shop. God had given them plenty of ammunition to back up their response.

As Todd and Nicole sat down later to discuss their decision with their son, they gave him both a biblical response and an expert's response. Knowing why this was so important to him, though, they gave him an out.

"Son, here's the deal. No, we are not going to sign for you get a tattoo now, and we've outlined the reasons why. If you will wait until you are twenty-five and you still want one, I'll pay for it," offered Todd.

"No matter how big?" their son asked.

"Ask me when you are twenty-five."

Yes, it was a gamble. Yes, they might later have to eat their words. But Nicole and Todd were willing to take a risk that their son would be more mature in eight years.

> Bottom line: Season your "no" with a pause, and you can avoid creating additional conflicts.

We are sometimes tempted to respond to our children's requests with a resounding "no" when the relationship would be better served by letting them know we will respectfully consider their requests. When our kids hit us with shocking requests that, in our minds, aren't even a topic for discussion, our natural tendency is to want to shoot the idea down immediately and move on to other things. We would be more successful at building the relationship if we would, instead, take the time to find out what is making them desire something that they most likely already know we won't feel is acceptable.

Fitting in is important to our tweens and teens. Whether they are on a softball team where everyone is bleaching their hair, a drum corps where kids are growing out their hair, a cheer squad where the girls are all wearing a lot of makeup, or a swim team where the guys are shaving their legs, our tweens and teens want to be accepted as part of the group. If we reject their requests without allowing them to be heard, conflict brews and our kids will feel disrespected and unheard. Even though we may say no to their request in the end, having their feelings validated will help them feel respected.

What About You?

☐ When have you responded with an immediate "no" to a request your tween or teen made and conflict occurred as a result?

☐ Nicole and Todd recognized that the relationship with their son was critical since he was close to going off to college. What were the steps they took to prevent what could have been a battle? Why were the steps important?

☐ Between you and your spouse, which of you tends to be more lenient? Does this cause difficulty between the two of you in your parenting?

☐ Which is more important, the family rule or the relationship? Why?

☐ In your home, are you moving toward dialogue that allows your tween or teen to feel your respect? What could you do to allow your child more opportunity for his or her own decisions?

☐ Consider reopening a dialogue with your tween or teen to talk through a time when there was conflict over your immediate "no" reaction. How would you start the conversation?

Pray with us:

Lord, there have been times when I've said yes or no too quickly without seeking Your direction. I admit that I react or overreact in ways that build walls between my child and me. Sometimes I know that I say yes because I don't want to disappoint them or because it is just easier even when I know it might not be the best thing for my child. Sometimes I've given in just because I'm tired or worn down and don't want the fight. Help me turn to You even when the answer is obvious in my mind. Help me treat my children's requests with respect, letting them know that I will need time to pray about it. I also pray that I will have the wisdom to engage my child's father in the process so that we can maintain a united front when the decisions really matter.

In Jesus' name,
Amen.

Dare 33 — MODEL FRIENDSHIPS FOR YOUR KIDS

Love is patient, love is kind. It does not envy, it does not boast, it is not proud. It does not dishonor others, it is not self-seeking, it is not easily angered, it keeps no record of wrongs. Love does not delight in evil but rejoices with the truth. It always protects, always trusts, always hopes, always perseveres. Love never fails. But where there are prophecies, they will cease; where there are tongues, they will be stilled; where there is knowledge, it will pass away.

—1 CORINTHIANS 13:4–8

Sydney stood in her kitchen watching the girls in the backyard play Capture the Flag with the boys. She had agreed to host the back-to-school get-together for her eleven-year-old daughter's class and enjoyed watching the kids indulge in ice cream and a fun game.

As she watched, however, her mind drifted back to her own childhood, and a dark memory resurfaced.

She remembered being on the school grounds, running with a group of girls her age, just like her daughter was now but with a different outcome all together. She absentmindedly touched her face as she remembered the blood that had run warm from the gash in her leg nearly as quickly as the tears had carved tracks down her cheeks that day so long ago.

A group of young girls had crowded around her, staring at her as she sat on the ground holding her bleeding knee.

One of them spoke. The rest of them laughed.

"Sssshhhh!" the leader had hissed at her. "They won't let us play if you don't stop crying! Get up and shut up!"

Missy was one of the popular girls, so she set the tone for the group. In a moment, all the others were chanting venomously, "Get up, shut up, get up, shut up!" at Sydney in a hushed whisper, so as not to draw the attention of the recess monitor.

Sydney had been the "tail" of the hand-holding line of girls playing Whip at recess. *Stupid game.* The object was to link hands in a line, then run in zig-zags around the grounds, trying to throw off the girl at the end. If you broke the chain, you ended up as the tail. Your personal goal was to get to the front of the chain, and then you got to lead which direction the chain ran.

Sydney had been flung off three times already. This last time she managed to slice open her leg on the gravel, and it was bleeding pretty badly. Her pride wounded at her lack of apparent skill and the absence of compassion from her schoolmates, she simply got up and walked away from the group, sitting down on a nearby bench.

Many other moments as memorable as this one peppered Sydney's childhood. She always seemed to be targeted for negative attention, catching the eyes of the bullies and stronger kids. The girls were difficult to connect with, cliquey, and for whatever reason, she didn't find a peer group to survive with until she was in high school. She steered clear of girls as friends for many years, lacking the ability to connect, deeply wounded by years of bullying and painful interactions that left her feeling inept.

Sydney's mind came back to the present, and she smiled in spite of the painful memories. As she looked outside at her daughter and her girlfriends, she knew her daughter had an entirely different experience than she did.

Sydney didn't know God when she was younger, but she was now sure that He had known her. After she met Him, she'd allowed Him to make her new. It was amazing how God had changed her heart toward women. Just as God gave Mary the blessing of female companionship in Elizabeth, He also gave Sydney that same blessing as she came to know Him more.

She had many women friends now who were a regular part of her life. Through the years, Sydney had come to realize that most women had a few things in common—they all suffered, they all persevered, and even when they didn't know what they were doing, they trusted God with the instructions and marching orders for the next thing. They shared tears, they shared laughter, and they shared prayers.

> Bottom line: Develop your friendships so your kids know what healthy ones look like.

Women and men need each other to do life well and to stay strong in their faith. Modeling this for our daughters and sons makes it easier for them to pursue relationships too. When the angel Gabriel told Mary that she'd become the mother of the Messiah, the next thing he did was send her to her cousin Elizabeth, who was older and also pregnant. They supported each other and found joy in their relationship.

God wired us for community. Even Christ chose twelve men to be in community with Him, and among those He had three friends—Peter, James, and John—whom He kept particularly close. Unfortunately, today's culture teaches us to be threatened by other women, and we often resist opportunities to create real, deep, and lasting relationships like God intended. But we need to choose to surround ourselves with women who will encourage us to do the hard thing. When we fail to do this, we are lonelier, and it takes much longer and is much harder for us to work out the things God wants in our lives.

What About You?

☐ How are you doing taking risks with other women? Did you do this study alone? If so, consider yourself encouraged to share what God has been doing with someone else by leading a group when you finish and/or sharing your experience with another individual.

☐ If you are doing this study with a group, consider the level of intimacy you've allowed yourself to experience with these women. Are you self-protecting? Are you oversharing? Have you found the balance between dominating a group because of low self-esteem and holding back because of fear of intimacy? Both are rooted in unhealthy perceptions of how God sees you. Consider spending some time on the "Who Am I?" page on NinaRoesner.com: http:// ninaroesner.com/who-am-i/.

☐ Have a humble and honest conversation with your kids about their relationships with others. Relationships are hard to navigate during the tween and teen years, and they need to guard their hearts without hardening them.

☐ Get to know your kids' friends. Send them affirming texts when something awesome happens. Let them know you are praying for them. Don't try to become friends with them; just get to know them and be a safe place for them. We love our kids well by loving their friends.

☐ Ask your closest female friend(s) to share two things with you: (1) a strength you have that she appreciates and how it affects your friendship; and (2) something that would help you be an even better friend to her. Want extra credit? Ask her if you have hurt her and then apologize, ending by praying for her and for your friendship. Be sure to thank her for being vulnerable and honest. Make it a safe experience.

☐ Ask God to reveal to you what your childhood friendships have taught you and how that spills over into your relationships with women today. Ask Him to reveal the truth to you, heal you, and confess any sin you discover in the middle of this listening experience with Him. Ask Him to change you and move forward in the way He directs.

Pray with us:

Lord, there have been times when I've been so hurt by other women that I shy away from friendship. I might go to Bible study or small group activities, but I'm afraid to get too close. That closeness might reveal my weaknesses, my inadequacies. I'll admit that sometimes I hold myself back because others seem to be above me: in looks, in intellect, in social status, or maybe I just don't feel worthy of their friendship.

God, sometimes I judge others, thinking them beneath me for all the same reasons. I've also judged some of the kids my own children are friends with. Help me bring glory to You by loving them well.

Forgive me if I am choosing to live life in a vacuum. Help me take risks with women relationally, knowing that I will be hurt, but help me continue to love well regardless. Teach me, Father. Help me remember that iron sharpens iron, and if I allow them to, friends can sharpen me. I know that I want good friends for my children. Please show me how to model this well for them.

In Jesus' name,
Amen.

Dare 34 — RESPECT THE RITES OF PASSAGE

"Fear not, for I am with you; be not dismayed, for I am your God. I will strengthen you, I will help you, I will uphold you with my righteous right hand."

—Isaiah 41:10 ESV

Do not let any unwholesome talk come out of your mouths, but only what is helpful for building others up according to their needs, that it may benefit those who listen.

—Ephesians 4:29

Danielle skipped to the car in the driveway, excited. "Yeah, I finally have freedom!" she screeched in sheer joy.

Nancy felt uneasy as she watched Danielle throw her swim bag, sunscreen, and sun visor in the backseat. She was concerned that her daughter was overly confident in her driving ability. It would be her maiden voyage, her sixteen-year-old's first time driving alone, and it would be on the interstate all by herself in what would most likely be bumper-to-bumper traffic.

"Lord," she prayed. "Keep her safe! Help me stay calm for the next thirty minutes while Danielle is en route to work. Please, just keep her safe. Why am I so antsy, Lord? It is just so hard to let go."

Nancy was working hard not to say all the things she really wanted to say. Things she had already said when driving with her daughter. Things like "don't go over the speed limit," "make sure you lock your doors," "look both ways," "stay in the slow lane," "be careful turning left out of the neighborhood," and "you know cars sometimes whip around that curve." She chose to remain silent about those nagging thoughts. She knew she needed to respect this rite of passage.

"Bye, honey! Be sure to text me as soon as you get to work." She plastered on the fake smile, trying to sound confident as she let her daughter go.

"I will, Mom. Don't worry. I'll be fine."

And off she drove.

As Nancy returned to the kitchen, Sam came in and gave her a quick hug. "Are you okay? I know that you don't think she's ready, sweetheart. But she needs a chance to grow up. She'll be fine."

Ten minutes later, Nancy was standing at the sink prepping dinner while Sam was working in the garage. All Nancy could think about was the conversation she and Sam had last night about Danielle's request to drive to work by herself. Sam was right. Other kids drove to work on their own all the time at the age of sixteen. She knew she was just being silly, so she chose not to press him further.

"I'll take care of it, Danielle," Sam said as he came in from the garage, obviously talking to their daughter on his cell phone. "You're sure you are all right to drive? Just be careful. I'll let Mom know. We'll look at it when you get home. Call us when you get there."

Nancy kept her feelings in check. She knew what she wanted to say to her husband, that she knew Danielle wasn't ready to drive alone yet. But she kept her tongue silent.

"What happened?" Nancy asked, trying to keep her voice calm.

"Danielle took out the neighbor's mailbox."

"Oh, Sam, is she okay?"

"She'll be fine. I think she is a little shaken up, but she'll be fine. I guess maybe she wasn't quite ready to drive by herself. It sounds like she hit a mailbox with the passenger-side mirror. It flipped forward, so there was no real damage to the car, probably just a little scrape. She must have told the neighbor that she'd have me come see the damage. She said she knew she'd have to pay for the mailbox."

"At least that's all that happened. I'm sure it will make her be more careful on the drive to work."

> Bottom line: Keep your fear in check, and you won't waste time worrying.

Ready or not, our tweens and teens are growing up, and we need to respect their rites of passage without fear and without smothering and over-parenting. For some parents, fear haunts us on a daily basis. We seemed to be wired to think the worst will always happen. When we recognize it, we need to know that we cannot control everything, but we do have a God who knows what is best and is in control. Can we trust Him with our kids? The truth is, according to research, literally 85 percent of the things we are worried about have either a positive or neutral outcome. Worry itself is a complete waste of time.

Our tweens and teens need to know that we trust them and respect them. Respect means letting go and allowing them to potentially make mistakes. Respect also means not stating the obvious to them. Once we've had the opportunity to teach our kids something, we don't need to constantly remind them how to do it as they walk out our door. Respect sometimes means keeping our mouths shut. In the end, they will make mistakes, but our job is to put wind under their wings that will help them soar to maturity.

What About You?

☐ What areas in your tween's or teen's life are you struggling to let go of? Why?

- ☐ Do you have a tendency to say "I told you so"? If so, what would be a better response?
- ☐ Sometimes we don't agree with the other parent's decision on freedom. Typically, dads are more willing to allow their teens more opportunity. Is this true in your family? If so, how can you combat your fear?
- ☐ Notice how Nancy faked her response to her daughter's good-bye. How might you have responded in a similar situation? Which is a better response?
- ☐ Notice Sam's calm response to Danielle. How do you think you might have handled the situation? What good came out of it? Do you think Danielle felt respected in the exchange?
- ☐ What was Nancy's response to Sam even though she was probably upset about the circumstances? What might have been your response to your spouse?
- ☐ Pretend you are sixteen again and heading out to drive alone for the first time. How would you have felt if your parents had responded like Nancy and Sam? What does that tell you about respect?

Pray with us:

Dear heavenly Father,

Your Word talks about setting an example for what is good and to teach integrity with our speech so that it cannot be condemned. May my responses to my children always be respectful so that they know I value them. My prayer is that I can show my husband the same respect even when we disagree about what is best for our children. Help me not to parent out of fear. Help me let go gradually at the right time so that I not only give my children opportunities for success but also opportunities to fail, strengthening them for adulthood.

Lord, help me recognize that You are in control of all things. Help me become aware of any fear-based thoughts in my parenting. Show me how to look at life through the lens of the Holy Spirit, knowing that You want what is best for my children and that Your desire is for me to parent toward release.

In Your Son's precious name,
Amen.

Dare 35 TEACH YOUR KIDS TO
SELF-PROCESS

*I will instruct you and teach you in the way you should go; I will
counsel you with my loving eye on you.*

—PSALM 32:8

*Eat honey, my son, for it is good; honey from the comb is sweet to your
taste. Know also that wisdom is like honey for you: If you find it, there
is a future hope for you, and your hope will not be cut off.*

—PROVERBS 24:13–14

*Therefore, as God's chosen people, holy and dearly loved, clothe your-
selves with compassion, kindness, humility, gentleness and patience.
Bear with each other and forgive one another if any of you has a griev-
ance against someone. Forgive as the Lord forgave you. And over all
these virtues put on love, which binds them all together in perfect unity.*

—COLOSSIANS 3:12–14

Sitting at the kitchen table shortly after dinner and cleanup were over, Ericka looked at Samantha, thankful she had chosen to take a walk after their last negative exchange that day. Samantha had been short-tempered and extremely harsh with her younger siblings most of the afternoon. Ericka had felt herself getting so frustrated and angry at her daughter that she was ready to scream. Instead of lashing out, though, she chose instead to take a walk and ask God what He had to say about the entire thing.

183

Verses from the Bible came to mind. "Love is patient, love is kind. . . . It keeps no record of wrongs" from 1 Corinthians 13:4–5. Then James 1:19 nearly did her in: "Be quick to listen, slow to speak and slow to become angry."

She thought of God's anger, of how long it took for His wrath to be ignited. She asked for forgiveness, thanked Him for His Spirit that had held her mouth shut, and thought through how she would deal with the situation.

"So, can you help me understand your attitude today?" Ericka asked her daughter later. "It seemed to me that I had to keep pulling you aside for the same discussion. The arguing, the disrespect with your siblings—you know what I'm referring to, right?" she calmly questioned.

"Um, yeah, I do. I don't know. I am really tired, I guess. I kept doing that, and I knew I was doing it. I'm sorry," the teen replied.

"Okay. Thanks for being easy to deal with on this. Do you know where you are in your cycle?" Ericka whispered to her daughter.

"Mommmmm . . . ugh. I think it's been, like, two months. Why?" She blushed.

"I don't mean to embarrass you, hon, and I know you aren't regular yet, but we need to control our emotions. We struggle with it our whole lives. PMS can totally not help," Ericka explained with a smile. "Anyway, I'll move on. So how do you think your brothers felt when you treated them like that?"

"Pretty bad, I guess. Angry, maybe? Hurt? Embarrassed because I did it in front of their friends?" came the reply.

"So what do you need to do?"

"Apologize?"

"And . . . ?" Ericka prodded gently, smiling and waiting.

"Oh, yeah, so, tell them how I would have felt if I were them and commit to not doing that again."

Home run.

"And how are you going to keep from doing it again?" Ericka asked.

"I'll need to pray. And try my best. But get help when I'm frustrated and don't know what to do. Am I grounded?"

"No, but you'll be doing their chores tonight. And I expect you to keep your word and apologize. Your brothers are as precious to God as you are and need to be treated that way. They look up to you too, because you are older than they are."

"They don't always treat me that way."

"You're right. Just so you know I will be having conversations with them too. I won't talk about what I'm saying to you now with them, and I'm not going to share what I say to them with you. That's respectful. But know I'm dealing with it, okay? I know I'm not perfect either, but when we all pray and get God's help to do our best, things just go better, don't you think?"

"Yeah, they do," came the reply.

"I love you," Ericka said.

Samantha smiled. "Love you too."

> Bottom line: Teach emotional intelligence by asking questions, and you will help your kids mature.

As our kids grow, it is important that we talk with them about their moods and their interactions with others. Tweens and teens sometimes have difficulty understanding their moods or how they are treating others. Offering up questions of self-discovery helps teens become more aware of their actions and what they are feeling. We need to teach them how to apologize to those around them and show them how to think more deeply so they can self-process in the future. Teaching them to take responsibility for their behaviors within the family helps build relationships. Parents who help their teens resolve conflict well create intimacy within the family.

What About You?

☐ How do you respond when you see your tweens and teens in a foul mood? What about when it starts impacting others in the house? What are you modeling in this area?

☐ If you have daughters, have you encouraged them to chart their cycles to become more aware of their moodiness? Why or why not? Do you think it might help?

☐ What about your own moods? Are you self-aware enough to let others know that you could use some grace on certain days?

☐ What steps could you take when you are frustrated and angry with your kids that would allow you to calm down enough to ask questions of your child?

☐ Have you taught your tweens and teens how to fully apologize? Do they share their regrets? Admit their fault? Restore the relationship? Tell the other person how they will change? Ask for forgiveness? How are you doing modeling this?

☐ How can you apply Colossians 3:12–14 from the beginning of this dare in your home?

Pray with us:

Lord, how can I teach my teens to become self-aware when sometimes I'm not even fully aware of my own shortcomings? I so easily snap at my kids when I'm frustrated with their behavior. Help me always to approach them from a position of wanting them to learn new responses rather than just harping on them for what they do wrong. Help me find my own quiet place to pray where I will find peace before engaging with my kids. Give me questions to ask that invite dialogue and help them think deeply.

Help me teach them to connect with others through apologies and resolving conflict well. Show me how to use these skills in my own life to build others up to serve You.

Thank You, Lord, for this opportunity to look in the mirror at my own behaviors. I know too well that sometimes what I see in my kids is a reflection of what they have seen modeled from me. May Your Holy Spirit within me prompt me to learn new responses myself rather than resorting to my own sinful behaviors. Thank You for growing me in this area.

In the precious name of Jesus,
Amen.

Dare 36 BE SENSITIVE TO OTHER PARENTS

"Praise be to the God and Father of our Lord Jesus Christ, the Father of compassion and the God of all comfort, who comforts us in all our troubles, so that we can comfort those in any trouble with the comfort we ourselves receive from God. For just as we share abundantly in the sufferings of Christ, so also our comfort abounds through Christ."

—2 Corinthians 1:3–5

"Do to others as you would have them do to you."

—Luke 6:31

Anita stood with her back to the sink drying her hands as Mitch devoured the last of his grilled cheese sandwich. She enjoyed these times of serving her seventeen-year-old even though dinner with the rest of the family had come and gone hours earlier. She loved the small talk that seemed to come at times like this—just the two of them alone.

"How was practice?" she quipped.

"Really good. Coach says I can start in Friday night's game," Mitch grinned. Before she could respond with enthusiasm, Mitch continued, "But, Mom, I'm really worried about AJ."

"What's up with AJ? I know it was really hard on him with you making the team when he didn't."

"Mom, AJ is making some really stupid choices. Not only is he smoking weed, but he's gotten into taking drugs."

"Oh, Mitch, I'm so sorry. Have you tried talking to him? The two of you have been friends since fourth grade."

"I've tried. He just brags about it to me and asks if I want to join him."

"Do his parents know what he's doing?"

"Yeah, they do now. He got caught at school yesterday with the drug bust. I have no idea what will happen to him now."

"Oh my," Anita replied. "I can't imagine what his parents must be going through."

As the conversation died down, Anita offered to pray with Mitch right there in the kitchen. "Lord, you know what AJ and his family are going through right now. I ask that you be with them in the midst of this chaos they must be dealing with. Calm their hearts and give Leah and Cal strength as they work through the legalities and issues they are facing. Use this situation to get AJ's attention and the help that he needs to work through his struggles. I also pray for Mitch. I know his heart is heavy at not being able to speak truth that could reach AJ's heart. My prayer is that you will give our family opportunity to provide love and support to this family in the trial they face. In Jesus' name, Amen."

A few days later as Anita was getting out of her car she saw Leah loading groceries into the back of her van. *Lord, this is an opportunity you've created. Be with me and give me the right words.*

"Hi, Leah. How are you?" Anita spoke in a loud voice so her friend would hear her across the parking lot.

"Good," Leah responded as she plastered a smile on her face. "How are you?"

"Things are going fairly well for us."

"Leah, we've been friends for a long time. I hope you don't mind me being direct, but I want you to know that Mitch told me what happened with AJ. I am so sorry for all you must be going through. I know this is something you probably don't want people to know about, so know that I haven't spoken a word to anyone. I just want you to know that I am here for you if you need to talk. When we were going through all our struggles with Peter, I would have given anything for a friend to share my frustrations. I felt so isolated."

Anita paused.

"Thanks, Anita. I'll admit this has been really hard. I just don't understand it."

"Leah, I can't imagine being in your shoes right now. Please know that we're praying for your family. How else can we help?"

"I don't know. We meet with an attorney on Friday."

"Why don't you come over for coffee tomorrow? If you don't feel like talking we could at least pray together. One thing I found I was doing when we were going through our struggles with Peter was that I was isolating myself. I felt I couldn't be around friends for fear of being judged as a parent. Leah, know that this isn't about you and Cal. This is about AJ. The best thing you can do right now is surround yourself with close friends who can help you stay sane through the insanity of the situation."

"Coffee and prayer sounds good. I guess you can probably relate to what I'm feeling. I'll stop over in the morning after I put the other kids on the bus. And thanks."

Bottom line: Be sensitive to others who may be struggling and be willing to be real so others can share their hurts too.

When it comes to parenting, often we can either find ourselves on the mountaintop or in the pit of despair. Rarely is parenting a steady, straight road with few bumps and turns. As women, it is easy to want to share when we are at the summit of the mountain. We want to share what is going well in our lives. "Look what God did" is an amazing story to tell; however, we need to also temper that with an awareness of when others are in the pit. Creating an environment where people are free to share their pain gives them hope and a shoulder to cry on. We want to live out Romans 12:15–17: "Rejoice with those who rejoice; mourn with those who mourn. Live in harmony with one another. Do not be proud, but be willing to associate with people of low position. Do not be conceited. Do not repay anyone evil for evil. Be careful to do what is right in the eyes of everyone."

This story could have turned out so differently if Anita hadn't been brave enough to enter into Leah's world of pain. Notice she did so by reminding Leah that she had walked a similar path with her son Peter. Many times we want to hide when we are going through painful experiences with our children. We're afraid to be real, because we choose to believe the lie that our children are a reflection of our parenting. We forget that God allows painful trials in our lives to stretch us. It is in the context of parenting that we sometimes grow the most. It is God's way of truly showing us that we are not in control, but He is.

As parents, we're usually eager to share when we are proud of our kids and their accomplishments. But we need to remember to be sensitive to where others might be emotionally with their kids before we start sharing. Our tongues can sometimes be a dart that could bring poison to others if they are not experiencing the same success. We also need to remember that our kids' successes are God's, not ours. It's fine to talk about those things, but we need to check our pride before opening our mouths.

Having a deep relationship with Jesus Christ destroys all barriers. It destroys separation and builds unity. When we focus on living our lives for the audience of One instead of other people, we rid our lives of fear and better represent God to the world. What we often fail to realize is that we are all on a journey, and at any given moment, we will be perceived as being in different places. Being brave enough to enter other families' lives when they are struggling displays the real truth that we are all essentially the same to God.

Precious. Wanted. Loved. Important. Being real and vulnerable allows others to remember that they are not alone.

What About You?

☐ Describe a pit that you've been in with your child. Were you able to share honestly with others? Why or why not?

☐ Anita bravely entered into what would undoubtedly be a painful dialogue with Leah. Do you think she did the right thing by approaching the conversation in the first place? Why or why not?

☐ What did Anita do that was effective? Could you be brave enough to enter into a similar conversation as she did? Why or why not?

☐ What did Anita do to connect with Leah? How might you have handled a similar situation?

☐ Take a look at your friends and the people you spend time with. Do the people you surround yourself with enter your world when things get tough? Based on this do you sense God wanting you to do something differently? If so, what?

☐ Anita could have told her friend Leah about Mitch's opportunity to be a starter in Friday night's game but wisely chose not to. How self-aware are you? When you find yourself with others, do you take into account how your words and actions might affect them? Are you sensitive to where they "really" are, not assuming all is well behind the "fake" smile? Being sensitive to others' situations shouldn't make us feel guilty but, rather, thankful. It should awaken in us a desire to love them, sharing what we have. As you look closely at each group of people you spend time with, ask yourself how well you know each of them. Are there people you know very little about? Do you know their struggles and yet do nothing? What specific things does God want you to do this week regarding this?

☐ Are you able to celebrate and mourn with those whose circumstances are different than yours? Why or why not? How has your upbringing influenced this? What are you modeling for your kids?

☐ What, if anything, took you by surprise in Anita's interaction with Mitch? What might you say about her heart as a mother and friend?

Pray with me:

Lord, give me sensitivity to what others might be facing when I come in contact with them. Sometimes I get so excited over the things that are going well in my life that I'm clueless to the pain others might be going through—especially in regard to their children. You tell us in Your Word to rejoice with those who rejoice and to weep with those who weep. Give me wisdom to notice when others around me might not be able to relate to my world. Help me care about others in a way that says when they are hurting, I too hurt. Show me how I can reach out to others so they feel comfortable being real when they are with me and so that I can help shoulder some of their burden.

Lord, help me not to buy the lie that I have nothing to offer. Help me be Your hands and feet to this world, no matter where I am or who I am with. Break me of any self-pitying, self-deprecating, or jealous thoughts that fail to esteem Your creation: people. Thank You for Christ's example of building relationships that know no race, wealth, status, or age.

In Jesus' name I pray,
Amen.

 *Dare 37* RELEASE YOURSELF
FROM WORRY

Be transformed by the renewing of your mind.
—ROMANS 12:2

*We take captive every thought to make it obedient to Christ. And we
will be ready to punish every act of disobedience, once your obedience
is complete.*
—2 CORINTHIANS 10:5–6

I can do everything through Christ, who gives me strength.
—PHILIPPIANS 4:13 NLT

Jill found herself dreading the weekends. As her kids had entered
middle school and high school, her stress level had risen to an
all-time high. They all had different places they wanted to go and
different friends to see, most of whom she didn't know. Jill knew she
was losing control of what her kids did, and she felt scared—scared
of what they might do, what they might try, or what might happen.

The stress typically started on Thursday after school. "Mom,
is it okay if I go to the movies with a group of kids tomorrow
night? Kelly said her mom could drive," her twelve-year-old, Ava,
would ask.

"Who is Kelly?" she would respond. "What movie are you planning to see? What's the rating?"

The conversation would continue until Jill found herself wanting it all to just go away. It was so much easier when she knew the parents and planned the movies they would see.

This week's stress began when Alex, her almost fourteen-year-old, came through the back door. The first thing out of his mouth was, "Mom, Jake, Ryan, and I are planning to go to the football game tomorrow night. Is that okay? Would you drive?"

Oh, the dreaded words.

It wasn't so much the driving that bothered her but the fact that they had invited Ryan. Jill knew Ryan had great Christian parents, but that kid was trouble. She had heard Ryan was doing snuff and popping pills these days. It scared her that Alex was still hanging out with him.

Jill barely made it through the conversation before her sixteen-year-old, Marissa, came strolling in from her flute lesson.

"Your siblings are already talking about the weekend. What are your plans for tomorrow night?"

"I'm not sure, Mom. A bunch of us were talking about hanging out at Tim's house after the game, but actually, I'm not sure I'm even going to the game. Evan said he might take me out to dinner at the new hamburger restaurant down by the river. We might just hang out. No worries, though. I promise to be home by curfew."

Jill would have to wait until after soccer practice to hear about Austin's plans. She knew he'd want the car, though, and that was plenty to make her edgy. It was all so stressful.

The next evening, after dropping the boys off at the football game, Jill stopped by her friend Beth's house to visit, since both of their husbands would be out of town until Saturday.

"Beth," Jill began. "How do you handle the weekends with your kids? I absolutely hate them now that my kids are older. I feel like I spend from Thursday through Saturday night worrying about what might happen. Now that Eva is in middle school, she is starting to hang out with girls I don't know. She wants to go to PG-13 movies, and I don't know what she is being exposed to or who these kids or their parents are. Then there's Alex. He's still a good kid, but there is one boy he hangs out with who makes me uncomfortable. I'm afraid he'll encourage Alex to make some stupid decisions. And," she continued, "Marissa has a new boyfriend. I've met him a couple of times and he seems to be a nice kid, but I know nothing about him really. Also, she's starting to want to go to other kids' homes for parties, and I have no idea if the kids' parents are truly home or not. Then there's Austin, who is driving now. I worry about him being out on the roads on Friday and Saturday nights. I know he needs to have some freedom, but there are so many terrible things out there." Jill sighed. "Now I know how my mom felt when we were all growing up." She let out a little laugh, though tears were on the brink of falling.

"Oh, Jill," Beth murmured. "This is really hard for you, isn't it?" Jill nodded her head.

"You mentioned your mom. Did she worry like this?"

"Of course. Don't you? Your kids are similar in age to mine."

"I'm sure I could head down that path if I allowed myself to. There's a lot to worry about when you have teenagers. But, Jill, isn't that what God's all about? Aren't we supposed to cast our burdens on Him?"

"Yeah, I guess so."

"Can I offer something up here? I know you might already know this, and I forget it myself sometimes when I have a lot going on with my kids . . . but when we worry like you seem to be, it's like we're not trusting God. You know God loves our children. Do you trust that He's in control and won't allow anything to happen that He is not aware of?"

"I guess I never thought about it like that."

"I was a little surprised the first time I thought about it too. Romans tells us to be transformed by the renewing of our minds.

What we think about controls us, Jill. It sounds like this is something that was handed down from a previous generation for you. If your mom's conversations are peppered with things she is worried about, I'm guessing you picked that up too as you were growing up. But I would encourage you to meditate on what God says about our thought lives. You may find a whole new perspective."

> Bottom line: Remember that what we pay attention to grows, and if you do you'll grow the right things!

Our thought lives can greatly influence how we parent, and if we aren't careful, those bad habits can be transferred to our children without our even realizing it. Taking our thoughts captive and renewing our minds can give us peace during the difficult parenting years and save our children from similar struggles.

Sometimes as parents we catastrophize what could happen by seeing only the worst possible outcome in everything. Worry impacts how we interact with our kids and can sometimes cause them to start worrying as well. We start making decisions based on what could happen rather than releasing our kids into God's hands. Good judgment in parenting still needs to prevail when it comes to putting boundaries around what our children do, but it is important to ease them into adulthood rather than keep them in a bubble until they are ready to leave the nest. Parenting is about allowing God to work in our lives to weed out the worry and fear, knowing that He is ultimately in control and will walk beside us when life gets difficult.

What About You?

☐ What things do you worry about in regard to your tweens and teens? Are those worries justified? Why or why not?

- [ ] What possibilities do you worry about that might have been part of a family legacy? Maybe a death of a sibling, an accident, a health issue, some other horrific event?
- [ ] What things does your spouse worry about that might be impacting your kids and your parenting? Where might those fears have originated?
- [ ] Do you often magnify the negative aspects of a situation and miss the good that is occurring? In what areas do you see that in your parenting?
- [ ] Do you allow yourself to run out a worst-case scenario? What can you do to stop yourself from imagining all the what-ifs?
- [ ] How do you feel about the concept of worry, fear, control, etc., being sin and a lack of trust in God? Can you remember a time in your life when you first started feeling these things? What do you sense God wants you to know about your childhood or your parenting that you haven't seen until now?
- [ ] Spend some time journaling over the next few days. Every time you have a negative thought involving fear or worry, write it down and ask God to reveal to you why you are being held captive to that worry or fear. Then write something you would like God to put in the place of worry or fear. Maybe you want God to replace your fears with hope or courage. Pray, asking God to help you release your concerns to Him, confessing your sin of control, fear, lack of trust in Him, etc., and ask Him to help you repent and heal in these areas.

Pray with us:

All-loving heavenly Father,

Help me remember that You are always in control. You love my children more than I do—and sometimes I wonder how that is even possible. I know that my fear is a reflection of my lack of trust in You. O Father, forgive me! Please heal me from this lack of faith. Help me understand where this fear is coming from. Is it something that has become a generational sin, or are there people in my life who breed this fear that seems to multiply like yeast in a mound of dough? Help me find the source so that with Your help I can root it out.

Psalm 119 says that Your Word is a lamp unto my feet and a light unto my path. Help me stay in Your Word so that I can learn to trust You more. Joshua 1 says that I am to be strong and courageous and that You are with me wherever I go. Help me remember that it is the same with my children—You are with them wherever they go.

In the name of Jesus,
Amen.

 **ENCOURAGE SELF-DISCIPLINE**

Rejoice always, pray continually, give thanks in all circumstances, for this is God's will for you in Christ Jesus.

—1 Thessalonians 5:16–18

You were taught, with regard to your former way of life, to put off your old self, which is being corrupted by its deceitful desires; to be made new in the attitude of your minds; and to put on the new self, created to be like God in true righteousness and holiness.

—Ephesians 4:22–24

Kiara caught herself picking up after her daughter yet again. The miscellaneous items that should have been put away were strewn about the house. Shoes here, scarf there, sweater over a chair, bowl from last night's popcorn on the coffee table. Frustrated, yet ready for the respite of a quiet house until her teen returned from school, Kiara chose to count her blessings as she began to pick up the trail of clutter.

1. Jasmine is doing well in school. *Thank You, Lord!*
2. Jasmine has a great group of friends—very much a blessing.
3. Jasmine is growing up to be a compassionate person. It was awesome to watch her interact with Aunt Martha last week.
4. I won't have her home for many more years, so I am thankful for our time no matter how frustrating.

And the blessing list continued . . .

As Kiara continued into the kitchen, she found herself pausing. "Lord, I know that Jasmine is a blessing, but sometimes she can also be downright frustrating!" She laughed as she said it.

Jasmine had torn through the house like a tornado this morning. She'd picked up cushions from the couch where she had done last night's homework searching for her calculator and left them wherever they fell, anyplace except where they should be.

"Found it, Mom. I'm sorry to leave you with the mess," she'd shouted as she ran toward the door. "I'll pick up this afternoon when I get home."

Right, Kiara thought, keeping a tight rein on her then-irritated tongue. *And when my Bible study group shows up this morning, I'll just tell them to sit wherever they can find a cushion or wherever there aren't popcorn kernels from last night.*

"Lord, she is such a good girl, and I know she has a lot on her plate with school and her after-school activities. Is this my role as a parent to pick up after her all the time? I love her so much that I would do absolutely anything for her. I might not always do it without complaining"—she chuckled—"but I would do anything for her. Show me the way, Lord. Either change my attitude and frustration or give me a different direction."

As Kiara continued to tidy the house for her group who would arrive in an hour, she felt God's gentle nudge.

Kiara, I want you to count the blessings I have given you, but I also want you to teach Jasmine how to take care of herself and others. You can't serve at church, in ministry in your home, and your family and serve all of them well if you are doing things others should be doing.

Tweens and teens need life balance. When their issues start impacting your daily life, they need a reminder that their behavior is not leading to independence.

"Thanks, Lord. I needed that today."

As Kiara pulled into the driveway later that day after picking up Jasmine from music lessons, she suggested that they spend a few minutes talking over a snack.

"Sure, Mom."

"Jasmine, I want you to know that I really am proud of the way you are maturing. You had such a gentle spirit with Aunt Martha last week. I loved watching the two of you interact."

"Thanks, Mom."

"You know that your dad and I want to teach you all the skills you'll need to be fully independent one day, don't you?"

Jasmine nodded her head in agreement between bites of trail mix.

Kiara continued, "It occurred to me this morning that you are starting to develop a habit that I think will not only impact you in the future but is impacting me right now. More mornings than not in the last three weeks, you've half-ransacked the house before you went to school."

"I know, Mom. I'm sorry. It's just that I don't want to be late for the bus. I don't want you to have to drive me to school."

"I appreciate that, Jasmine. But you are leaving me with a mess just about every morning these days. We need to find a way to change that."

"Mom, I've told you I will clean it up as soon as I get home, but by the time I get here you've already done it. You really can save it for me."

"Jasmine, I live in this house too. I have friends who stop by during the day while you are gone. I like to sit on the couch for my quiet time. Do you really think I can enjoy my time with God if I have to look at the mess all around me? One morning a week I'm hosting Bible study here. I don't want to spend time cleaning that morning when it should already be done. I've been thinking about this, and I am wondering if the problem is that you've not gathered your things together for school the night before? Could that be it? I'd like you to work hard at picking up snacks or whatever you've left in the family room the night before, and maybe even consider getting your school stuff completely packed before you go to bed. Do you think that could help?"

"I might have to go to bed a few minutes later; it takes about twenty minutes to get everything ready for the next day."

"I can be flexible with that to start, but after two weeks, I want you to build that into your routine so that you're ending homework in time to be in bed by ten. You will have to figure out how to do both."

"I guess so. I can try that."

"Okay. So let's plan on this then. Can you set an alarm on your phone to remind yourself? I want you to be successful. If it happens again, there will be a consequence."

"A consequence? You've got to be kidding!"

"Jasmine, the consequence is intended to help you not forget the rule the next time. Just know that from here on out, there will be no more morning tornado through the house. I know that might seem harsh, but our job as parents is to help you become a balanced adult. I just don't want you to be stressed out and develop the habit of always being in a rush. I know that's what you want as well. Keep the family room picked up in the evenings, and there won't be a problem. I love you, Jasmine. I know you'll do better, baby. I'm more than willing to give you a gentle reminder in the evening if that will help."

"Okay, Mom. I'll try to do better. The alarm on my phone is a good idea."

"That's great, honey."

> **Bottom line:** Don't rescue but instead equip, and all involved will become more mature.

Sometimes we allow other people's behaviors to negatively impact us. We find ourselves in situations where we are playing catch-up from other people's messes (literal and otherwise) instead of modeling self-respect and helping our family members have life balance. Rather than create potential conflict or add stress to our kids' lives, we bail them out, often because it's easier and takes less time than teaching them good habits. But it also doesn't allow them to grow and frequently gets in the way of other commitments we have made.

God intends for us to serve; He doesn't want us to be selfish. But He also doesn't want to exhaust us. Rather, He wants to bring us up in the discipline of His Word. If we will focus on God's blessings for us and stay plugged into His way of thinking, He will bring to mind very specific guidance and verses to help us make the right choices. This means discernment is always the high order of the day.

Self-discipline and self-awareness are things parents often struggle with practicing themselves, much less developing in their children, due to the hurry-up world we live in. But in the long run, it is more helpful if we take the time to model these things now and be mature, which leads to more maturity.

What About You?

☐ Go back through the dialogue, and look for decision points. Step outside the content, as if you were on a balcony, and watch the dialogue play out on the stage below. Look at the activity of the communication (i.e., positive feedback, asking questions, self-control, etc.). Where could things have taken a different turn?

☐ Many times a short blessing count will help us move from being angry or hurt to being objective about a situation. How are you doing counting your blessings with regard to your children? Set a timer, and take five minutes to list the things you see in your kids that you are thankful for.

☐ What things are you doing that your tweens or teens should really be taking care of themselves?

☐ Pick one of those things to have a dialogue with your child about shifting the responsibility to him or her. How will you start the conversation?

☐ Spend a few minutes taking a self-inventory. What are all the reasons you might have chosen not to address these areas? Is there any fear attached to it?

Pray with us:

Gracious Father,

My prayer is that You will give me eyes to see the areas where my children need to grow toward maturity and help me find ways to spur them on. Sometimes it is easier to overlook their negligence because I want to love them well and know that they are just kids. Lord, help me remember that I'm working toward the goal of having them be responsible adults and doers of Your Word. Open my eyes, Lord, to the things I need to pass on to these children. Help me teach them the skills they need while being sensitive to the person You designed them to be. Help me focus on the character traits that You reveal in Your Word. Give me strength to press on toward the goal to win the prize for which You have called me.

In Jesus' name,
Amen.

Dare 39 **POINT OUT WHAT IS RIGHT**

Finally, brothers and sisters, whatever is true, whatever is noble,
whatever is right, whatever is pure, whatever is lovely, whatever is
admirable—if anything is excellent or praiseworthy—think about
such things. Whatever you have learned or received or heard from me,
or seen in me—put it into practice. And the God of peace will be with
you. I rejoiced greatly in the Lord that at last you renewed your concern
for me. Indeed, you were concerned, but you had no opportunity to
show it. I am not saying this because I am in need, for I have learned
to be content whatever the circumstances. I know what it is to be in
need, and I know what it is to have plenty. I have learned the secret of
being content in any and every situation, whether well fed or hungry,
whether living in plenty or in want. I can do all this through him who
gives me strength.

—Philippians 4:8–13

Milan had just finished mowing the lawn when his mom, Lashonna, walked out to inspect his work. Overall, he'd done a great job. The grass wasn't blown onto the sidewalk or the street, and he had even remembered to mow the small patch next to the garage. As she noticed a swath of grass that he had missed, however, she recognized an opportunity.

"Hey, thanks for mowing the yard!" she began. "I appreciate how you did it without complaining. You paid attention to detail and got that tricky little spot by the garage, and you kept the grass off the sidewalk and street! Thanks so much! You are developing a keen eye for details!"

"Thanks, Mom," he replied, grinning.

"You bet. When you are reliable like this, it makes me trust you more. Hmm . . . Say, does that look right to you over there?" she asked, pointing to the patch he'd missed.

"Oh, I missed that over there. I'll get it before I put away the mower," Milan said.

"Okay, no big deal. Thanks for doing this for the family," she said, walking back toward the front door.

> Bottom line: Indirectly point out opportunities for improvement, and you will teach respect and build self-esteem.

As parents we want to teach our kids to take inventory of the work they've done and instill a sense of ownership in their accomplishments. All too often our natural instinct is to point out what they missed or compare their work with what they've done in the past, rather than thanking them for what they did today that was good. Finding opportunities to build our kids up rather than tearing them down is critical. By asking questions that allow them to find their own mistakes without making them feel stupid, we show respect relationally, which calms the fight-or-flight response that usually ensues when we point out their shortcomings.

What About You?

☐ Go back through the brief conversation between mom and son. Find each small decision point, and look at what the mom did and what she did not do. How could this situation have been handled poorly? How did she keep it from being a negative interaction?

☐ Put an elastic band around your wrist today. Each time you catch yourself allowing judgment, criticism, or complaining to come out of your mouth, snap it. Choose today to only speak words of blessing to others, focusing on things that will build them up. As you talk to yourself today, keep the same rule. This is not an exercise in delusional thinking but rather an activity that will help you see how negative or positive you are naturally.

☐ If you haven't started your gratitude notebook yet, tonight is a great time to begin by writing three things you are thankful for about each of the people closest to you. Cultivate this thankful heart practice before bed each day, and you will find your ability to see what is good improving.

Pray with us:

Dear precious Lord,

Help me have an attitude of gratitude when I interact with my children. Even though they might not always do things up to my standard, help me teach them with grace and mercy. Give me words to help them thrive rather than words of judgment, criticism, or complaint. We all want to feel respected, and I want to show my children acceptance for who they are as people. All this time I thought parenting was about teaching them, but I'm coming to realize that You gave me these children to teach me. Help me become a reflection of You in all my relationships. Thank You for who You are becoming in my life.

In Jesus' name,
Amen.

Dare 40 BE A RELATIONSHIP ARCHITECT

Therefore encourage one another and build each other up, just as in fact you are doing.

—1 Thessalonians 5:11

She brings him good, not harm, all the days of her life.

—Proverbs 31:12

Felicia's husband, Kent, was a project kind of guy. He carefully thought through what he wanted to accomplish each evening and almost every weekend. Mow the lawn, trim the bushes, paint the siding—he tackled his list in the same manner he handled his day job: with tenacity.

The neighbors all raved about how nice the house always looked. His boss told him regularly how much the organization valued him. The church liked having him on committees. Felicia loved that he was so accomplishment driven. In fact, that's one of the reasons why she married him.

What she didn't realize came with all this, though, was the way she would have to give Kent at least a few days' notice if she had something to do on a Saturday and would need him to watch the kids. Oh, he was more than willing to take the boys to do something fun or play with them in the backyard. They would have a great time together! It just needed to be on Kent's schedule. As long as he could still get something "accomplished" during the day, everything was good.

Over time, Felicia began to realize that they needed to work together to master the schedule if there was going to be any family connection time. Kent had not grown up with a family who played together. Spontaneity didn't come easily.

Now that the boys were hitting puberty, Felicia knew that her early encouragement for Kent to have relationship with the kids was paying off. She could honestly say that the little boy in Kent was finally having a chance to bloom, and her boys were the beneficiaries of his many talents. As she watched her men get in the car to head to the tennis courts, she remembered well a discussion that had taken place several years prior with a dear friend.

"Felicia, you need to be his cheerleader! You need to give him permission to take a day off work. You need to thank him for all the hard work he does. Thank him for the projects he does around the house. Then ask him what fun things you can plan for the family. Kent doesn't think that way. You need to help him think of fun things to put on the list."

What wise counsel she had received.

Felicia became the master family scheduler with Kent's permission. "I know you want to connect with the kids," she had offered. "Let me help you plan so you know you not only have time to get things accomplished around the house but you can have confidence that your boys will have a relationship with you as they grow older. I promise to let you know the plan well in advance."

He agreed, and she put the schedule in motion. Once a month he had a two-hour block of time to do something special with each of the kids, and they scheduled family fun time at least once a week.

Sometimes the boys' time with Kent took no planning, like biking through the park or going to get ice cream. Other times she would encourage Kent to get involved with the boys doing what each of them enjoyed. Brad liked video games, so Kent would spend time playing with him. It obviously wasn't Kent's thing, but it helped him know what was going on in Brad's head. Nick was into baseball, so they'd go to the park and work on catching fly balls. Luke was still at the stage of loving the animal world. Together they'd go down to the creek to catch tadpoles, and at Kent's suggestion, they had built an outdoor terrarium for Luke's turtles, mixing Kent's love for accomplishment with Luke's excitement for turtles.

When Kent and the boys returned from their tennis match, Felicia fondly watched the boys run upstairs, trying to see who would make it first to the shower. She put her arms around Kent and looked in his eyes. "Honey," she said. "Thank you for being such a good dad and connecting with the boys! I'm so glad I married you."

> Bottom line: Help your husband connect with the kids, and your family bond will strengthen.

Typically females are wired for connection more so than men. That's why it's important for moms to be relationship architects in their homes, creating opportunities for connection for everyone. Since most men are the primary breadwinners, they might not see the need for emotionally connecting with their tweens and teens as much as we do. If we can find ways for our husbands to be involved while still being able to get their own needs met, our children will reap the benefits. Create opportunity through encouragement. Be his cheerleader!

What About You?

☐ What is your husband's relationship with the kids? Does he do work beside them? Play with them? Interact with interest in their worlds?

☐ In what ways do you need to encourage interaction between

your husband and your kids? If you are divorced, could you encourage this interaction with their biological father?

☐ In what ways have you created one-on-one time between you and your children? What about promoting one-on-one time with each child and their dad?

☐ What interests does your husband have that you could get your children involved in as well? What interests do your children have that they could participate in with your husband?

☐ What do you think becoming a relationship architect in your home might look like?

Pray with us:

Lord, Your Word says that we are to encourage one another daily. Help me encourage my husband in his role as a dad, and help me work with my children to give them an understanding of the importance of relationship as well. Help me take my role as a relationship architect in our home seriously, so that we can love each other well and be a light for You. I love how Your Word models relationship for us by encouraging time to connect, time with our heavenly Father, and time for rest. My prayer is that when all is done, You will say to me, "Well done, my good and faithful servant."

In Jesus' name,
Amen.

NEW BEGINNINGS

And let us consider how we may spur one another on toward love and good deeds.

—Hebrews 10:24

These forty dares might be over, but we all know that parenting is a journey that never ends. There are always opportunities for our growth as we interact as a family. As our kids get older, new problems emerge that will show us where we need to change in order to maintain a healthy relationship.

But before you go, let's circle back around a bit. It is time to revisit the self-assessment we did back in Dare 1. As you look at those pages in this book, take a moment to put a star next to the points you've worked on. What tangible improvements have you made since then? What are you doing differently since you completed this the first time? Resist the temptation to focus on the areas where you are lacking, and instead give yourself some grace and view the list through the lens of the Holy Spirit, specifically Philippians 4:8–13.[1]

If you have been walking this journey with another woman or a small group, take a few moments to jot down the growth you've seen in your partners—and share it with her or them.

Now that we've had forty days of journeying together, you have new stories. Pick what feels like an achievement for you. It might be the smallest, most insignificant event to a stranger but represents a shift in thinking for you. Describe the single moment in time that means the most to you as evidence of God's work in your life. Start with answering the following questions:

- Who was there?
- When did it happen?
- Where were you?

Then tell the "what" of the moment. End with your own bottom-line statement that gives advice to someone else. Share this story within your small group or, if you're doing the book alone, share it with another family member or friend.

Now think through each of your children, focusing on their strengths and opportunities for growth. Think of a recent story that represents each kid's strength. Sit down with them individually, and let them know what you love about how they are maturing.

Take time to thank God for these wonderful children He has given to you to help you mature in Him. Read aloud Psalm 103 giving God thanks for all He has done. We see this not as an ending, but rather as a beginning for you and your family.

We encourage you to continue to spend time interacting with other parents on this journey. You might even want to go through *With All Due Respect* again, focusing on another child or trying it with a group of moms and dads combined. If you are brave, you might want to start a new group of dare-takers. Lead, pray, and support them through the forty dare process to not only help other women grow spiritually and in their parenting, but to continue your own growth.

Know that we would love to interact with you in our e-course or have you share a story on our website at www.greaterimpact.org. You'll also find helpful resources there, like a set of questions for both mom and dad if you choose couples' study and our small group guide to enhance your experience. We'd love to hear about your journey and growth. We also have a prayer team that will pray for your parenting struggles.

Another option to help you grow in your parenting is our

parenting course, Generations™, from which *With All Due Respect* was adapted. We have begun videotaping this program for small group use, and it should be available soon. Check out our website for more details.

Note: We are collecting stories for Debbie's blog at www. DebbieHitchcock.com. Feel free to e-mail your story to us at information@GreaterImpact.org. We may include your story in an upcoming post or book, or maybe we will contact you to share it in our Generations™ video parenting course!

ACKNOWLEDGMENTS

Debbie and I could write volumes about the hard work of so many people who brought this project to life. We are both well aware that none of this would have been possible without them, and frankly, are concerned we'll miss someone. First and foremost, we want to thank Jesus Christ, our Lord and Savior, for creating our families, and for binding us all together. May You be pleased with what has been created here. We are also very thankful for the reader—you put your trust in us as you struggle on this parenting journey. We want you to know we're not worthy of that trust, but God is. Please know we are not perfect, and it has been our prayer from the beginning that any good which emerges from this book be credited right back to God. It is our intention to do His work and stay out of His way. If you have questions or concerns or comments, please contact us through our website, as we deeply desire to engage with you as you struggle. This parenting path, like marriage, is often a road paved in tears. You are not alone.

We want to thank David Shepherd, our agent, who has been patient beyond measure with the arrival of the book concept. His time, prayers, encouragement, and wise counsel have brought this book into being what it is. We deeply value him and are thankful for the opportunity he has provided to us.

Much appreciation to the awesome staff at Thomas Nelson Publishing. We have had absolutely nothing but positive interactions with you all! Even when questions or disagreements arise, they are so easy to work with because we are all on the same team.

Specifically, to Brian Hampton, publisher at Thomas Nelson, your belief in us blows me away and we promise to work hard supporting what God's creating here. Kathie Johnson, administrative assistant, we've been told you run the show! THANK YOU for all the things you do that we're not even aware of. Jessica Wong, senior acquisitions editor, you are brilliant and your attention to structure will make this book a better experience for the reader. Your availability for questions and advice made everything better. We are grateful. Heather Skelton, senior editor, your attention to detail, writing skills, personal contact, and desire to make this book awesome have resulted in a work that makes Debbie and I both look like we're writers. I'm guessing that was no small feat. You are a blessing and we're so thankful! Jeff James, vice president of marketing and Stephanie Tresner, marketing manager, your enthusiasm for getting the book out there is appreciated—we promise to do our part supporting it! Tiffany Sawyer, publicist, your efforts launch this project in a way we couldn't do on our own. We know how hard you work and we're so appreciative! Kristen Gathany, art director, we just want to say we think you are brilliant. The cover creation process was awesome and we admire what you've done. Seeing the book on the shelf makes us smile and think of you!

Debbie and I also want to thank a number of other really important people, folks that no one knows just how much they've impacted the creation of *With All Due Respect*. The list is long, and suffice it to say, all our friends and family have been a part of this in some small way! Specifically, however, we do want to mention a few.

Pastor, author, and friend, Chad Hovind—The wisdom you bring from the pulpit of Horizon Community Church and the material you've shared in numerous areas of our ministry bless many. Thank you for your continued investment in us.

Pastor, friend, and Gottman certified counselor, Dick Lehman— Your authenticity as a pastor, a dad, and your vulnerability in sharing your stories and encouragement have impacted not only our personal parenting in our families, but the content of this book. Thanks for helping us create relationship with our kids.

Christian counselor, Rebecca Buckalew—You have consistently equipped both of us with wisdom, perspective, and prayer support as we parent our own kids.

The many moms who have been real in sharing their struggles with us—We've enjoyed many lunches and coffees as we've cried and prayed for our children together. Thank you for not only being vulnerable but encouraging us in making this material available.

Bonnie Hauer—you are our prayer warrior, coleader in ministry, and awesome friend who encourages us and is graciously flexible as "the book" monopolized meetings and cropped up in random unrelated discussions. We love that you are part of our leadership team of three. Your wisdom generates great dialogue and keeps us focused on what really matters!

Greater Impact's Titus 2 Army of Women—You've helped us with encouragement, prayer support, a few details here and there, and lots of positive pressure for continued forward movement in our writing. We especially appreciate April Bock—You gave us feedback on a number of the dares and gave us encouragement to "hurry and get this project finished." Thank you. We also want to thank Charlyn Elliott—Your insight on topics for a few dares made this book so much better.

Debbie Collins—You prayed intentionally for this project from the beginning, that God's hand would be on it and His will would be accomplished. You have been a friend and supporter of our ministry for years and we just love you to pieces.

Dale Robertson—A Greater Impact board member and trainer for Generations™. Thank you for your insight and vulnerability in speaking to dads.

Brandon Little, pastor of Landmark Ministries—You trusted us enough to speak to parents through video having no idea where this project would go. May God richly bless you as your message reaches more people through the parenting course, Generations™.

Shaunti Feldhahn—Your research and excellent parenting materials have made a difference in both the Hitchcock and Roesner families. What He has created through you is truly remarkable and groundbreaking. Families are changed by your work and we highly recommend your books. Your work definitely helps our ministry make a Greater Impact!

To those who have dared to take Generations™—We've laughed together, cried together, and prayed together. May His truth shine through you in your parenting! Thanks for being brave and transparent. To God be the glory!

ABOUT THE AUTHORS

[[Save two pages]]

NOTES

DARE 4: PUSH THE RESET BUTTON

1. 2 Chronicles 1:10 "Give me wisdom and knowledge, that I may lead this people."

DARE 8: TAKE CARE OF THE TEMPLE

1. http://www.babycenter.com/0_ending-the-chore-wars-8211-how-to-get-your-mate-to-help-on-t_1425647.bc.

DARE 12: PARENT WITH PERSPECTIVE

1. Genesis 2:18 "The Lord God said, 'It is not good for the man to be alone. I will make a helper suitable for him.'"

2. Matthew 7:3–5 NKJV "And why do you look at the speck in your brother's eye, but do not consider the plank in your own eye? Or how can you say to your brother, 'Let me remove the speck from your eye'; and look, a plank is in your own eye? Hypocrite! First remove the plank from your own eye, and then you will see clearly to remove the speck from your brother's eye."

3. Genesis 2:24 NKJV "Therefore a man shall leave his father and mother and be joined to his wife, and they shall become one flesh."

DARE 13: LEAP OUTSIDE YOUR COMFORT ZONE

1. http://goodmenproject.com/featured-content/empathy-gendered-brain-7-things-men-women-need-know-hesaid/

DARE 19: OFFER COMPASSION INSTEAD OF JUDGMENT

1. Jeremiah 10:23 "Lord, I know that people's lives are not their own; it is not for them to direct their steps."

DARE 21: TAKE TIME TO LISTEN

1. Ephesians 5:24 "Now as the church submits to Christ, so also wives should submit to their husbands in everything."
2. Ecclesiastes 4:9 "Two are better than one, because they have a good return for their labor."

DARE 24: TALK YOUR KIDS THROUGH DISAPPOINTMENT

1. Ecclesiastes 3:1–8 "There is a time for everything, and a season for every activity under heaven: a time to be born and a time to die, a time to plant and a time to uproot, a time to kill and a time to heal, a time to tear down and a time to build, a time to weep and a time to laugh, a time to mourn and a time to dance, a time to scatter stones and a time to gather them, a time to embrace and a time to refrain from embracing, a time to search and a time to give up, a time to keep and a time to throw away, a time to tear and a time to mend, a time to be silent and a time to speak, a time to love and a time to hate, a time for war and a time for peace."

DARE 25: DROP THE COMPARISONS

1. Proverbs 22:6 NKJV "Train up a child in the way he should go, and when he is old he will not depart from it."

DARE 29: RESPOND WITH CALM

1. Shaunti Feldhahn, *For Parents Only*, (Colorado Springs, CO: Multnomah Books, 2007), 28–29, 102–103, 122.

DARE 30: REMOVE THE MASK

1. Galatians 6:2 "Carry each other's burdens, and in this way you will fulfill the law of Christ."

NEW BEGINNINGS

1. Philippians 4:8–13 "Finally, brothers and sisters, whatever is true, whatever is noble, whatever is right, whatever is pure, whatever is lovely, whatever is admirable—if anything is excellent or

praiseworthy—think about such things. Whatever you have learned or received or heard from me, or seen in me—put it into practice. And the God of peace will be with you. I rejoiced greatly in the Lord that at last you renewed your concern for me. Indeed, you were concerned, but you had no opportunity to show it. I am not saying this because I am in need, for I have learned to be content whatever the circumstances. I know what it is to be in need, and I know what it is to have plenty. I have learned the secret of being content in any and every situation, whether well fed or hungry, whether living in plenty or in want. I can do all this through him who gives me strength."

CPSIA information can be obtained at www.ICGtesting.com
Printed in the USA
LVOW08s0446060416

482349LV00001B/1/P